CONTENTS

Published 2010. Pedigree Books, Beech Hill House, Walnut Gardens, Exeter, Devon, EX4 4DH.
books@pedigreegroup.co.uk | www.pedigreebooks.com
Written by Rachel Elliot | Photographs © FremantleMedia, Ken McKay and Jack Davis.
Pedigree Books would like to thank Jack Davis, Jessica Morris,
Katrina Morrison and Susan Wilks for their help in compiling this book.
Copyright © FremantleMedia Limited 2010
The X Factor is a trademark of FremantleMedia Limited and Simco Limited.
Licensed by FremantleMedia Enterprises. www.xfactor.tv

talkback THAMES   SYCO tv   FREMANTLEMEDIA   Pedigree

THE X FACTOR

THE GREATEST LIVE SHOW ON TV

PRESENTING YOUR FINALISTS!

£12.99

This year has produced some of the most incredible talent ever seen at audition stage. Our official Annual is your guide to all things *X Factor*. Relive the drama of the auditions, the tension of Bootcamp and the pressure of the Judges' Houses stage. Decide who you believe deserves to win in 2010, go behind the scenes and discover how to cultivate your own star quality!

Join the Judges as they scour the villages, towns and cities of Britain for the next international phenomenon. And remember, this year you are the fifth Judge!

THE JOURNEY

For the twelve finalists and the four wildcards, their audition is only the beginning of a testing time that will challenge their determination, self-belief and talents to the limit.

Stage 1: Auditions

Each auditionee faces Simon Cowell, Louis Walsh and Cheryl Cole, for the first time. With just one song, they must convince the Judges that they have the potential to be a superstar.

Stage 2: Bootcamp

Those who passed their auditions face an exhausting challenge. They must sing and perform to keep their dreams alive, while the Judges whittle their favourites down to just thirty-two.

Stage 3: Judges' Houses

Each Judge is given a category to mentor and spends individual time with their assigned acts. After evaluating their potential, the Judges each choose three finalists to represent them in the live shows.

Stage 4: The Live Shows

The twelve finalists and the four wildcards now face the toughest Judge of all – you! Every week they sing for a place in the show. The two acts with the lowest public vote must sing again. Then the Judges decide who deserves to stay in the competition.

YOU ARE THE FIFTH JUDGE!

Who do you think has the extra magic needed to be a global superstar? To be a Judge, you have to know what to look for from the moment an auditionee walks onstage. Check out our exclusive judging tips:

Preparedness:

A good contestant must work hard and spend lots of time rehearsing. How well has the auditionee prepared for this moment?

Likeability:

Listen to the audience – do they like the auditionee? It's really important to see how the crowd reacts.

Style:

A sense of personal style shows individuality and self-belief. Has the auditionee thought about his/her outfit, hair and makeup?

Attitude:

A combination of self-confidence and respect is a great mix. What does the auditionee's conversation tell you about him/her?

Presence:

A good performer should own the stage. Does this auditionee grab your attention?

Performance:

A successful performance is relaxed, confident and exciting. Is the audience on its feet? Have you got goosebumps?

Talent:

Most importantly, does the auditionee have genuine talent? Staying in tune, keeping in time with the music and making the song uniquely his/her own version are all vital factors.

Confidence:

A certain level of confidence is essential for a great audition. Does the auditionee have eye contact with the Judges? Is he/she a cool cat or a frightened rabbit?

FINDING THE X FACTOR

It's the question that's on everybody's lips. What *is* the 'x factor'?

If you're planning to audition for the next series of *The X Factor*, you'll be up against some pretty tough competition. You have to stand out from the crowd.

It's important to think about every aspect of the image you're presenting to the Judges. In the following pages you'll find hints, tips and tricks of the trade to help you be the best you can be.

Use this information as a guide to help you bring out your own unique qualities so that everyone can see and appreciate them.

REMEMBER, YOUR AUDITION PREPARATION STARTS NOW!

Paije Richardson

Cher Lloyd

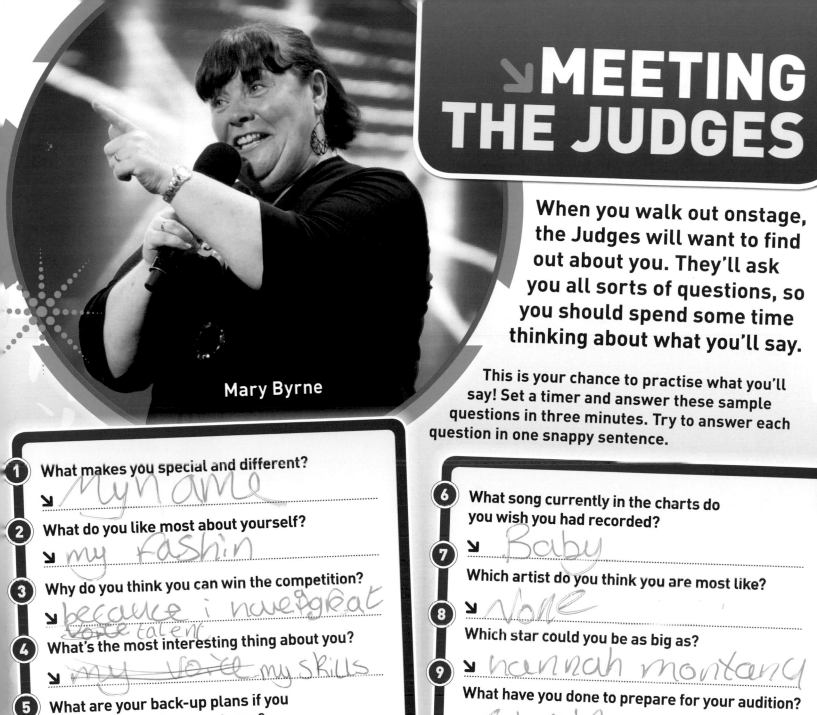

↘MEETING THE JUDGES

When you walk out onstage, the Judges will want to find out about you. They'll ask you all sorts of questions, so you should spend some time thinking about what you'll say.

This is your chance to practise what you'll say! Set a timer and answer these sample questions in three minutes. Try to answer each question in one snappy sentence.

Mary Byrne

1 What makes you special and different?
↘ *My name*

2 What do you like most about yourself?
↘ *my fashin*

3 Why do you think you can win the competition?
↘ *because i have great ~~voice~~ talent*

4 What's the most interesting thing about you?
↘ *my ~~voice~~ my skills*

5 What are your back-up plans if you don't become a famous singer?
↘ *be a writer or a actress*

6 What song currently in the charts do you wish you had recorded?
↘ *Baby*

7 Which artist do you think you are most like?
↘ *None*

8 Which star could you be as big as?
↘ *hannah montana*

9 What have you done to prepare for your audition?
↘ *Singin*

10 What would you call your first album?
↘ *megar star*

↘ PREPARATION

Being well prepared is the key to giving a fantastic audition. You'll have a lot to think about in the weeks leading up to your audition, so it's a good idea to write a checklist to remind you of the details.

X Factor Check List

Get vocal training

Choose songs

Rehearse

Pick an outfit

Audition!

Leona Lewis - Series 4 Winner

Daniel Fox

VOCAL TRAINING ↘

A good vocal trainer can teach you all sorts of vital skills. You'll learn how to use your vocal cords properly and how to breathe while singing, as well as how to cope with the challenge of performing onstage.

Remember, your aim is to find out what your voice is capable of, not how to sing like someone else. Some people worry that getting vocal training means their individual singing style will be changed. Vocal training won't change your voice – it will strengthen it and enable you to sing more effectively. It'll help you to find the 'x factor' inside yourself!

KNOW YOUR VOICE

It's massively important to know your vocal range. That means identifying the highest and lowest notes that you can reach in your normal singing voice, without straining. You should never force yourself to hit a note that's outside your vocal range.

Male singers should find out whether they are a bass, baritone, tenor or countertenor. Female voices are usually soprano, mezzo-soprano or contralto. A vocal trainer will be able to tell you this.

Every singer has a different tone, and it will really help your audition to know what your tone is. For example, it might be soft or it might be sharp. You'll then be able to pick songs that suit your voice, and that will impress the Judges.

Lauren Francis

Yuli Miguel

Karl Brown

"SUPERSTARS being created!"

Dannii

JLS
Series 5

BREATHING EXERCISE

Try this exercise in bed in the morning and before you go to sleep at night. It will show you the difference between taking a 'normal' shallow breath and breathing fully and deeply.

1. Lie down flat.
2. Put your hands on your sides.
3. Take a slow, long breath in and imagine that it's filling up your stomach. You should feel your stomach rise and your sides and chest expand.
4. Breathe out slowly, counting up to five.
5. Repeat steps 1–4 five times.

PREPARATION

SONG CHOICE

Choose songs that you know really well and feel comfortable with. You must memorise the words and be able to sing with or without a backing track. Picking a song that suits your voice is vital.

You should also think about your age and personality when choosing your song. Sing something that reflects who you are and the kind of music you would like to make. Your song should be challenging for you, but should show off the things you do best.

Choose a song that you can sing without straining your voice. Record yourself singing the song and listen to it with a critical ear. Try to notice the places where your voice sounds strained or uncomfortable.

Remember, you might only get to sing part of your song, so avoid songs with long instrumental openings.

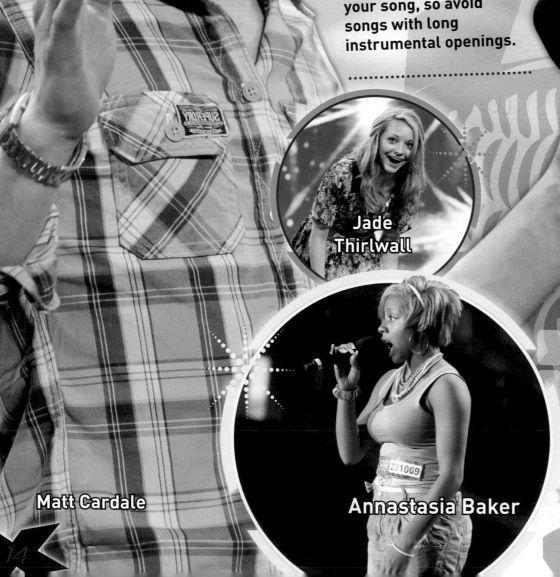

Matt Cardale

Jade Thirlwall

Annastasia Baker

MEMORY TIPS

Do you find it hard to remember the words to your chosen songs? The obvious solution is plenty of rehearsing, but here are a few tips to help you memorise the lyrics.

- Read and repeat small sections of the song at a time, so you learn it piece by piece.
- Tape yourself singing the song, and listen to it every day.
- Write out the words of the song several times.
- Associate each word with a picture in your mind.
- Read the words of the song every night before you go to sleep.
- Play the song softly as you go to sleep.

Harry Styles

DICE

Cyril Grant

POSTURE

Good posture will help you to be a better singer, so it's worth finding out more about holding your body correctly. You should stand naturally with your head, neck and shoulders loose and relaxed. Hold your head up, keeping your chin level, especially when singing very high or very low notes. Keep your muscles as relaxed as possible and try to make your movements easy and flowing.

SINGING EXERCISE

1. Stand with your shoulders relaxed and your arms hanging loosely by your side.

2. Breathe in as slowly as you can.

3. Sing a single note and hold it for as long as you can without becoming short of breath. Do not suck in your stomach.

"JUST RELAX yourself."

Simon

Daniel Pearce Series 6

Alexandra Burke Series 5 Winner

PREPARATION

PRACTICE MAKES PERFECT

You should be super-familiar with your song choices, so whichever song the Judges request, you can perform it to your best ability.

It's not good enough to arrive only knowing a couple of lines – although this has happened! Knowing all the lyrics will help boost your confidence.

Regular singing practice will not only help you to be familiar with your songs; it will also train your voice and help it to become a perfect instrument.

Rebecca Creighton

Myles Blair

Diva Fever

221277

10627

DICIPLINE

It takes extremely hard work, determination and focus to be a successful singing star. You're going to need bags of discipline to succeed, and that starts right now at your first audition.

LISTENING

To learn about singing, it's a good idea to listen to a wide range of different voices. Don't just listen to your favourite music. Play songs from various genres and think about how the singers are achieving their unique sound.

RELAXATION

Being stressed and worried can really affect your singing, so if you know that you panic under pressure, learn some relaxation exercises that you can do backstage to keep yourself calm.

CHOREOGRAPHY

Keep your choreography to a minimum. The Judges are there to listen to your singing voice, not to watch you dance. Leaping around the stage may distract them or, worse still, annoy them.

You don't need wild, jerky movements to add expression to your performance, but neither do you want to look like a frozen statue! A few simple hand motions will make you look at ease with being onstage. If you're not sure what to do with your free hand, hold it loosely by your side.

Watch past auditions and look at how the successful applicants stood and moved. Write down everything you notice, and pay special attention to any Judges' comments about choreography.

Stephen Hunter

Remember, every move you make will affect the sound you are trying to produce, so keep it simple.

Underground

" You just need **MORE CONTROL**"

Pixie

Damien Devine

WARM-UP EXERCISE

Before performing a warm-up exercise, loosen up your whole body. Deep breathing and yoga exercises may help with this. Above all, don't strain your voice while you're warming up.

1. Stand up straight and take a few long, deep breaths.

2. Sing 'Ha-ha-ha-haaa' in a middle range that's comfortable for your voice.

3. Notice your diaphragm supporting the sounds.

Blush

166025

166024

GROUP HARMONISING ↘

In some ways, singing in a group is even harder than singing solo. You have to work very hard to blend your voice with that of another singer or singers. The performance depends on every single person in the group. You all have to blend in with each other.

Remember that when you're singing in harmony, no one person should stand out. The melody is the most important thing. Practise in a circle so that you can all hear each other.

HARMONISING EXERCISE

1. Identify your audition song's melody. Make sure that you can sing the melody on pitch.

2. Listen out for the instruments that are being played in harmony with the song's melody. It won't be easy at first, but keep trying and you will succeed.

3. Try to blend your voice with the instruments or you could sing two or three notes above and below the melody. Keep trying until you find the harmony.

4. Record yourself as you practise and listen back to the results.

"You need to work on YOUR HARMONIES."

Cheryl

Husstle

F.Y.D.

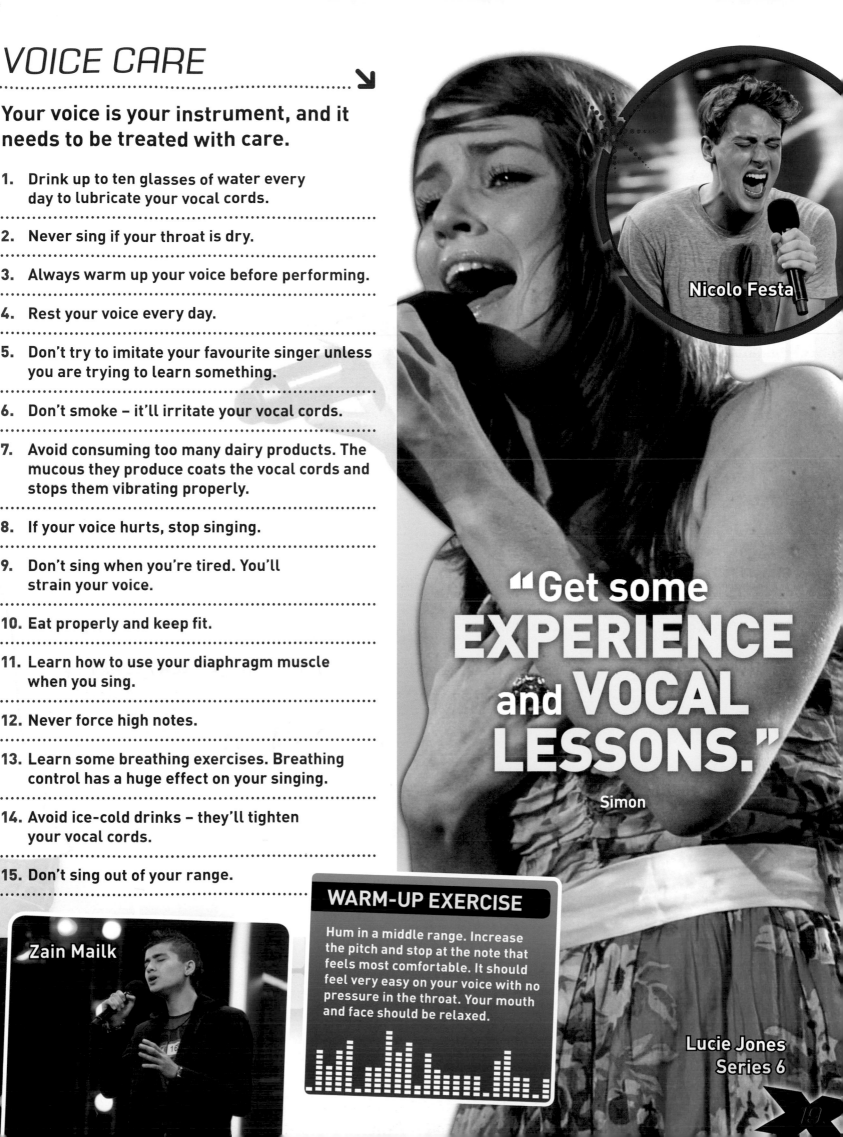

VOICE CARE

Your voice is your instrument, and it needs to be treated with care.

1. Drink up to ten glasses of water every day to lubricate your vocal cords.

2. Never sing if your throat is dry.

3. Always warm up your voice before performing.

4. Rest your voice every day.

5. Don't try to imitate your favourite singer unless you are trying to learn something.

6. Don't smoke – it'll irritate your vocal cords.

7. Avoid consuming too many dairy products. The mucous they produce coats the vocal cords and stops them vibrating properly.

8. If your voice hurts, stop singing.

9. Don't sing when you're tired. You'll strain your voice.

10. Eat properly and keep fit.

11. Learn how to use your diaphragm muscle when you sing.

12. Never force high notes.

13. Learn some breathing exercises. Breathing control has a huge effect on your singing.

14. Avoid ice-cold drinks – they'll tighten your vocal cords.

15. Don't sing out of your range.

Nicolo Festa

"Get some EXPERIENCE and VOCAL LESSONS."

Simon

WARM-UP EXERCISE

Hum in a middle range. Increase the pitch and stop at the note that feels most comfortable. It should feel very easy on your voice with no pressure in the throat. Your mouth and face should be relaxed.

Zain Mailk

Lucie Jones
Series 6

YOUR IMAGE

You may have a fantastic singing voice, but your image is important. People make a lot of judgements about you before you even open your mouth, so it's vital to make a good first impression on the Judges and audience.

Spend some time before your audition deciding what your image should be, and how to use your appearance to tell the Judges something about yourself.

OUTFIT

Whatever you wear for your audition, it should feel comfortable and suit your personality. Think carefully about your outfit and what it says about you.

Gamu Nhengu

Yuli Minguel

Fiona Robertson

FASHION DOS & DON'TS

- Don't choose anything uncomfortable – you're probably going to spend a lot of time waiting around before your audition.

- Do wear something that makes you feel attractive and that you know suits you.

- Don't go overboard. An outlandish costume is just a way of hiding your true self, and the Judges are looking for people who feel comfortable in their own skin.

- Do pick an outfit that fits with the moods and themes of your song choices.

- Don't be a fashion victim. Choose clothes because you like them, not because your favourite celebrity wears them.

- Do one rehearsal in the outfit you intend to wear for your audition. Make sure you can move and breathe easily in it.

- If you're planning to wear high heels, do make sure that you can walk gracefully in them.

Katie Waissel

FASHION TIPS

- Choose clothes that make you feel good when you put them on. If you feel good, you look good.

- Know your body shape and understand what suits it – and what doesn't.

- Ask a trusted friend for honest advice about what suits you and what doesn't.

- Choose clothes that show off your best features.

- Remember, confidence is the most attractive and appealing thing that you can wear.

STYLE PICKER

It's important to make your style your own, but here are just a few tips to get you started in the right direction. Do any of these styles jump out at you? Circle those that fit best with your personality. Then turn the page to find out more about them.

GLAMOROUS

GOTHIC

EMO

ROCK

URBAN

BOHEMIAN

CLASSIC

GIRLY

Tom Richards

Don't forget, these are just a few examples of the array of styles you can choose from. Pick and mix from all fashions until you have created a look that's uniquely you.

YOUR IMAGE

CLASSIC

Bring a touch of class to your surroundings. A classic style is clean, neat and well groomed. Colours, accessories and fabrics are understated. Think fitted jackets, crisp white shirts and clean lines.

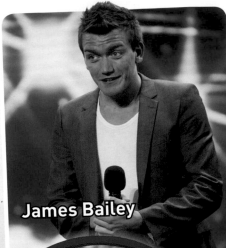

James Bailey

GOTHIC

Black is back! The gothic look is all about dark, gloomy colours like black, navy and burgundy. Think vampires, swirling mists and mysterious castles. To achieve this image you could dress all in black, dye your hair black and use black make-up. Shoes and boots should be heavy and chunky, and accessories should be metallic.

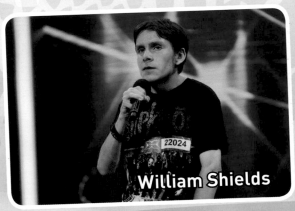

William Shields

Indigo Rose

**Diana Vickers
Series 5**

BOHEMIAN

The bohemian style is all about freedom and creativity rather than designer labels. Think loose tunics, tousled hair and floating skirts. The bohemian look embraces a mixture of patterns, colours and fabrics – totally unique and individual.

- Amber jewellery
- Anklets
- Bold tribal patterns
- Braces
- Brooches
- Chunky bracelets
- Duffel coats
- Embroidered clothes
- Ethnic, dangling earrings
- Feathers
- Floaty tunics

- Floppy hats
- Fringe boots
- Gladiator sandals
- Hats
- Headbands
- Headscarves
- Jeans
- Large silk scarves
- Layered accessories
- Long beaded necklaces
- Long dresses
- Long knitted scarves

- Loose tunics
- Minimal make-up
- Peasant shirts
- Peasant skirts
- Rainbow colours
- Rolled-up sleeves
- Sandals
- Sideburns
- Straight-leg trousers
- Thick belts
- Tousled hair
- Wooden beads/pendants

EMO

Emo fashion doesn't have a rigid code, but there are definitely things that are cool and uncool. Band logos play a major part in this – just make sure that the bands are cool!

- Band T-shirts
- Black eyeliner
- Fingerless gloves
- Hoodies
- Knee socks
- Layering long-sleeved T-shirts
- Lipgloss
- Messenger bags
- Simple, flat shoes or boots
- Skinny jeans
- Stripes
- Thin, long crocheted scarves

Ross Barron

King Captain

GIRLY

Girls just want to have fun! This look is ultra-feminine, with frills, bows, lace and ruffles accentuating every outfit. It's all about high heels, sparkles and sequins. Use pretty belts to cinch in your waist and don't be shy about accessorising – this look is all about enjoying fashion!

Lorraine Clark

URBAN

Hip-hop never goes out of fashion. Think thick gold chains, baggy trousers and baseball caps for guys, while girls are wearing large hoop earrings, eye-catching outfits and thick platforms.

Pierre Lafayatte-Marsh

Tanja Elder

ROCK

A genuine rock look should be edgy and bold. Focus on creating an image that's totally in line with your music. The rock look has a laid-back vibe that implies you've either just finished a gig, or you're about to jump onstage!

- Black leather jackets
- Black T-shirt
- Boots
- Checked shirt over a white T-shirt
- Dark shirts
- Dark sunglasses
- Drainpipe jeans
- Funky patches and badges on bags and clothes
- Red lipstick
- Skinny belts
- Studded belts
- Vintage band T-shirts

Jamie Archer
Series 6

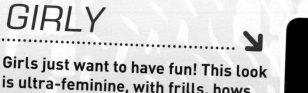

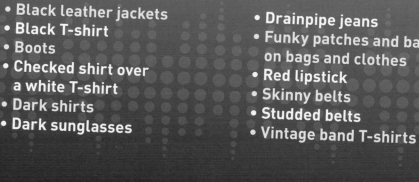

YOUR IMAGE

GIRLS HAIR

Think of your hair as part of your outfit. The perfect hairstyle will give the finishing touch to your image. If your hair looks and feels right, it'll give a big boost to your confidence.

Olivia Phillip

BOB

Sharp, shiny bobs are massive this year. They're great for showing off beautiful bone structure and a slender neck. You can wear them back-combed with flicked out ends, or blow-dry them under with a round hairbrush.

Remedy

Francesca Leigh

LONG AND WAVY

Long and wavy hair looks natural, beautiful and is hugely versatile. With different textures, lengths and partings, no two hairstyles will be the same.

K Dollz

PONYTAIL

Classic ponytails are hitting catwalks all over the world. Worn high they look fun and worn low they look elegant.

UP-DO

Putting your hair up can add height, glamour and style to any outfit, whether you're wearing a ballgown or a pair of jeans.

Barbara Allen

COLOUR

Kirsty Crawford

If you enjoy changing the colour of your hair, you'll know what a powerful impact it can have. Rich, natural-looking brunette shades are right on trend. If you prefer a statement colour, bold berry colours will give your look the edge.

1940S GLAMOUR

Think of the glamorous film stars of Hollywood's golden era. Waved hair that falls below the shoulder teamed with a side parting will recreate the classic look of the past.

Laura White
Series 5

CHIGNON

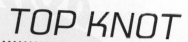

A chignon is a classic low bun that sits at the nape of the neck. It can be smooth or messy, depending on the look you're trying to create.

Muriel Acheampong

TOP KNOT

This look is young and fun, and just like the chignon you can make it sleek or messy.

Rebecca Ferguson

HAIR TWIST

You can twist all your hair at once, or twist smaller strands and pin them around your head to create an interesting, vibrant image.

Fiona Calley

PIXIE CROP

A pixie crop with a brow-length fringe, swept to the side with a little hair gel, is a slick, smart look. It suits any outfit, image or mood.

Marie Neil

I Candy

FRINGES

This year, keep a short back and sides and focus your creativity on your fringe. Longer fringes give loads of styling option. It's all about texture!

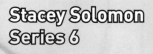

Stacey Solomon
Series 6

YOUR IMAGE

GUYS HAIR

Guys' hairstyles this year are inspired by a bygone era of classic elegance.

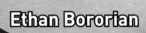
Ethan Bororian

PARTINGS

Alex Ko

The most important thing is to find a parting that suits your face shape. A classic side sweep, for example, can look really elegant, but it has to work with your bone structure.

SLICK BACK

Your hair will have to be cut in a way that allows you to slick it back. Use hair wax and experiment with different directions before the day of the audition.

Josh Moore

SHORT AND SPIKY

Short styles don't have to be boring. Depending on the cut, a short style can be exciting and versatile.

Sebastian Tarlem

COLOUR

For guys, golden blond gives a super-sharp look to an edgy style.

Lloyd Daniels Series 6

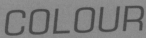
Louis Tomlinson

LAYERED

The different lengths of layers can help to create amazing hairstyles. Choose the hair length you want and add a few layers. Personalise your image with a side-swept fringe.

Amy Harman

SCENE AND EMO HAIR

Both Scene and Emo hairstyles are vibrant, cool and colourful, with short sides and choppy, long fringes. The Emo style generally prefers black, while the Scene style uses brighter, fun shades like red and purple.

Razor cuts, long layers, bobs and bowl cuts are on trend for the girls, while guys should try a shaved style, multiple hair sections or cropped hair with coloured strands.

Above all, remember that these haircuts are not meant to be perfect. They're all about showing your creativity and edginess. So go for it!

Nu Status

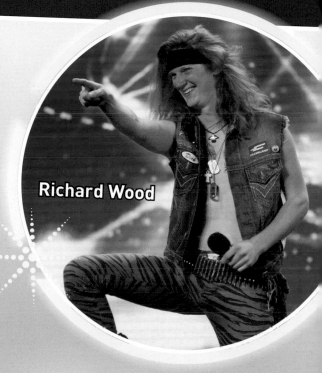

Richard Wood

HAIR DOS & DON'TS

- If you're in a band, check what the others are doing with their hair.

- Do brush or comb your hair every day.

- Don't comb your hair when it's sopping wet.

- Let your hair dry naturally at least once a week.

- Do use a gentle shampoo.

- Don't change your hair colour the day before your audition.

- Do get your hair trimmed every six weeks.

- Do shampoo your hair daily.

- Don't use styling products too often.

- Do try out your hairstyle before the day of the audition, and take some photos of yourself in your chosen outfit.

John & Edward
Series 6

Sophie Isaacs

195403

YOUR IMAGE

MAKE-UP

You'll want to look your best under the lights onstage, and make-up will help whether you're male or female. Your face isn't going to be the reason you pass the audition, but the Judges will appreciate the fact that you take pride in your appearance.

Cher LLoyd

Diva Fever

Katie Waissel

Leona Lewis
Series 3 Winner

MAKE-UP TIPS: GIRLS

- Avoid anything that makes your skin look shiny – shimmer powder will not look as flattering on camera as foundation with a matte finish.

- Choose eyeshadow and blusher shades that are a little stronger than your natural colour.

- Use a brow pencil to darken your eyebrows if necessary.

MAKE-UP TIPS: GUYS

- Use a tinted moisturiser to keep your skin looking healthy and even-toned.

- The combination of stress and hot lights may make your face look really shiny. You can guard against this by using anti-shine powder.

- You can use concealer to hide dark circles under your eyes.

BEAUTY DOS & DON'TS

- Do work out a regular care routine for your skin.

- Do use a muslin facecloth to clean your skin.

- Do use a moisturiser that contains sunscreen.

- Don't risk getting sunburn. It's very damaging to your skin.

THE NATURAL LOOK

1. Use foundation to even out your skin tone and create a good base.
2. Dust on a little pink powder, topped with bronzer.
3. Add a thin layer of mascara.
4. Finish the look with a little clear lipgloss.

Julia Collins

Kim Howlett

Lucie Jones
Series 6

STYLE SECRETS

The Judges will be on the lookout for something totally new and different during the auditions. We've brought together the hottest fashion trends for you to use as a guide. Now it's up to you! Pick out the details that will suit your personality and create the look of 2011.

GIRLS

Antique-style fabric
Boyfriend blazers
Camel coats
Capes
Flowing dresses ✓
Hair bows ✓
High hemlines
High splits
High waists
Knee socks
Lace ✓
Lingerie as outerwear
See-through fabric
Soft blouses
Thigh-high boots ✓
White tights ✓
Wide leg trousers

GUYS

Airforce styles
Army green
Army styles
Bow ties
Sack suits
Three-piece suits
Warriors

BOTH

Buttoned-up collars
Futuristic styles
Leather ✓
Metallic fabric
Patterned fabric ✓
Stripes
Velvet

Chrissie Pitt

Justin Vanderhyde

Jade Peters

↘ ON THE DAY

The build-up to your audition will be stressful, tiring and challenging. You'll have lots to organise and remember, and you'll be feeling a whirlwind of emotions.

The way you handle the build-up to your audition is really important. If you get through to the next stage of the competition, things are only going to get more stressful!

Sweet Chilli

Storm Lee

THE NIGHT BEFORE ↘

The evening before your audition, follow these steps to ensure that you are relaxed, well prepared and happy.

1. Take some time out to focus your thoughts about tomorrow. Find a space where you can be alone. Think through your song list and the sort of things the Judges might ask you.

2. Do a final check of your outfit and accessories, and make sure that you have prepared everything that you are going to take with you to the audition.

3. Relax with your family or friends over a healthy meal. Try to avoid watching TV – chat or play a game instead.

4. Have a warm bath with plenty of bubbles.

5. Get an early night.

6. Don't forget to set your alarm!

EARLY START

On the morning of your audition, have an invigorating shower rather than a bath. Eating well is important so a large, healthy breakfast will give your body the fuel it needs to get you through the day. You'll be burning up a lot more energy than usual.

Allow yourself plenty of time in the morning to do your make-up and hair, and to get into your chosen outfit. Then ensure that everything you need is packed and remember to do a final check and leave the house on time ready for the day ahead.

BE PREPARED

If you're a fan of the show, you're already aware of how fierce the competition is. There will be some exceptional singers, so you need to make sure that you are as well prepared as you can be.

Make sure you take everything you might need with you on the day. Write a list and tick off each thing as you add it to your bag. Here are a few ideas to get you started.

X Factor Check List

- Large bottle of water ☑
- Snacks ☑
- Backing tracks ☑
- Make-up ☑
- Hairbrush / Comb ☑
- Pocket mirror ☑
- Headache pills, just in case ☑
- Any notes you have made ☑
- A book to read while you wait ☑
- Pen and paper ☑

Keri Arrindell

Amy Morris

John & Edward Series 6

FINDING THE FACTOR

↳ON THE DAY

TRAVEL PLANS ↘

The one thing that's guaranteed to stress you out is arriving late for your audition. That's why making travel plans in advance is so important. You should aim to make the day of your audition as stress-free as possible.

If you're travelling by train or bus, check the timetables in advance and plan to arrive at the venue early. Allow a little extra time for unexpected problems and delays. Use the travel time to go over your audition in your mind and practise some relaxation exercises.

If you're travelling to the audition by car, work out the route you're going to take and allow plenty of time in case of traffic jams. Check the radio traffic bulletins regularly to help you avoid problems.

If you get travel sick, don't forget to take a remedy with you!

Stacey Solomon
Series 6

JUDGES' QUESTIONS ↘

You have already spent some time thinking about the sort of questions the Judges are likely to ask. Another thing they might ask about is your journey to the venue. Take out your pen and paper and write a few words about your day so far. Think about anything funny or unusual that happened on the way.

BE FRIENDLY

When you arrive at the venue, you'll meet a lot of other auditionees. Take this opportunity to make some new friends. They will understand exactly how you are feeling, and chatting to them may help to calm you own nerves.

Even if you are naturally shy, make yourself smile at people and introduce yourself to them. After all, you have something in common with them all – you love music. You may make lifelong friends, get some good tips from people who have auditioned before, or even meet singers who'll be interested in starting a group.

Remember that this day is bristling with opportunities. Be on the lookout for them and seize every interesting chance that comes your way. The truth is that you can make your own luck.

"We want to see YOU!"

Geri

Twem

AUDITION DAY TIP

There will be lots of new faces around you, and afterwards it may be difficult to remember who was who if all you have are names and phone numbers. While you have a pen and paper in your hand, write descriptions of the people you have made friends with. Make notes about where they are from and what you talked about.

ON THE DAY

FOCUS

A short while before your audition, find a quiet space and spend a little time by yourself. After the excitement of travelling to the venue and meeting new people, you will probably need to regain your focus before going onstage.

Read over your song choices again, and do some breathing exercises. Think about why you are there and what you hope will happen in your audition.

Now visualise yourself walking confidently onstage and singing better than you have ever sung before. Tell yourself that you are going to do well and be successful. Having a positive mental attitude will help you to make your dreams a reality.

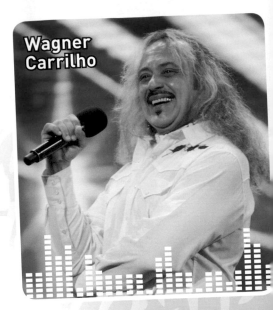

Wagner Carrilho

OUR PREPERATION TIPS

Make up your mind to have fun and enjoy the day, no matter what the outcome.

Don't drink fizzy drinks on the day.

Drink lots of water throughout the day to keep your vocal cords lubricated and your body hydrated.

Keep some healthy snacks in your bag and eat at regular intervals.

Liam Payne

Mary Byrne

Jordan Williams

Alexandra Sherry

SAVE YOUR VOICE

Amy Louise Aldred

While you're waiting to audition, try to avoid practising. You will hear lots of other auditionees going over their songs, but don't be tempted to overwork your voice. You need to save it for the audition.

You have been preparing for this day for a long time, so have faith in yourself and trust that you're ready. Don't allow other people to knock your confidence.

Start doing your vocal warm-up exercises about half an hour before you are due to perform. This will give your voice ample time and will enable you to sing to your best ability.

Check your hair and make-up before you go onstage.

Don't panic if other auditionees are planning to sing the same song as you. Stick to your plan.

Don't be afraid to ask questions if you are unsure about anything on the day.

Try to avoid air conditioning before your audition.

You should be as relaxed as possible for your audition, so arrive early to avoid your stress levels rising because you're watching the clock.

Daniel Pearce Series 6

Aiden Grimshaw

Emily Pearson

John Adeleye

Alexandra Burke Series 5 Winner

35

FINDING THE **FACTOR**

↘ # THE AUDITION

At last the moment has arrived – it's your big chance and you don't want to blow it. In the next few pages you'll read about what to expect when you walk onstage, and how to cope with the emotions you'll experience.

You have been working towards this audition for a long time, so focus all your nerves and all your energy on making this the best performance you have ever given. **GOOD LUCK!**

Marlon McKenzie

Joe McElderry
Series 6 Winner

BE YOURSELF ↘

It sounds obvious, but the Judges are there to listen to you, not to watch a tribute act. Don't be afraid to give your own interpretation of a well-known song. The Judges are looking for something new and original.

Some auditionees even write new lyrics for old songs. Of course, this can backfire too! But if you believe in your talent and practise hard, the Judges will appreciate your commitment, energy and effort.

Gamu Nhengu

ACTING CONFIDENT ↘

The Judges want performers who look as if they belong onstage and feel completely at home there. Even if your nerves are making you shiver and shake, learn a few tricks of the trade to look cool and laid back!.

- Research some breathing exercises and use them to relax you before your performance.

- Know your lyrics inside out.

- Walk onstage with your head up and your shoulders back.

- You will seem more confident if you look straight at the audience and smile as you walk across the stage.

- Say hello to the Judges and make eye contact with them.

- Answer the Judges' questions clearly and honestly.

- When you're singing, try to make eye contact with the Judges and with a few people in the audience.

- If you make a mistake, keep going as if it never happened. It is more professional to be able to carry on.

- Smile!

Olly Murs
Series 6

FIRST STEPS ↘

One of the floor crew will direct you to a marked spot on the stage where you have to stand. This is the place that the cameras will be set up to film, so it's important to stay in that area. Take a deep breath, walk over to the marked spot and say hello to the Judges.

JLS
Series 5

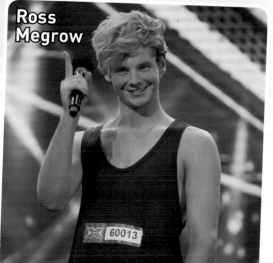

Ross Megrow

60013

George Bieknell

THE AUDITION

Laura Bennett

SPEAKING TO THE JUDGES

Before you sing, the Judges will spend a few minutes chatting to you and asking you questions. That's why it's such a good idea to think up a few answers to obvious questions in advance.

Being onstage can make you forgetful, starstruck and tongue-tied, so it will really help to come prepared. Of course, the Judges are sure to ask you something unexpected. Here are a few last-minute tips to help you keep your cool.

- The Judges want you to do well. Don't be scared of them.

- Imagine that your best friend is beside you, holding your hand.

- If you find yourself stammering, pause, take a deep breath and start again.

- Listen carefully to the question you are being asked.

- Be honest and open in your answer. The Judges want to meet the real you.

COPING WITH CAMERAS

If you're not used to being onstage, it can be quite disconcerting to have all those lights and cameras pointing in your direction. You might even find that smaller cameras are moving around you during your audition. Try to ignore them, you should be able to focus on your song without being distracted.

If you feel relaxed and confident enough to sing to the camera, don't do it all through your performance. Always remember that you are auditioning for the Judges and the audience. Focus on giving your best possible performance.

The Reason

John Wilding

Alistair Nwachukwu

JUDGES' CHECKLIST

What are the Judges really looking for? What makes the perfect auditionee? Above all, of course, they want to find someone with talent. But there are lots of other factors that will affect how successful you are at audition. These are some of the elements that make up the perfect auditionee:

Geneva Lane

Judges' X Factor Check List

- Sounds unique and isn't just trying to copy other artists.
- Has self-confidence without being cocky. ✔
- Is willing to learn. ✔
- Has obviously worked hard to prepare for the audition. ✔
- Shows good manners. ✔
- Looks relaxed and at ease onstage. ✔
- Is willing to listen to constructive criticism. ✔
- Has determination and ambition. ✔
- Understands the modern music scene. ✔
- Is able to identify artists who have been a big influence. ✔
- ✔

Treyc Cohen

Adrian Bumbescu

THE AUDITION

USING A MICROPHONE

Try to get some experience of using a microphone before your audition. It will help you to learn that you don't have to strain your voice to reach the back of the auditorium. Allow the microphone to be loud for you.

Nial Horan

Sinead Henderson

Jeffery Lawerence

Danyl Johnson
Series 6

COPING WITH SURPRISE

When you're onstage, there's always the potential for something to go wrong. The backing track might not work. There might be a problem with the sound or the cameras.

If you are stopped in the middle of your performance and asked to wait or start again, don't panic. The worst thing you could do would be to lose your focus or your energy. Keep thinking about your dreams and goals. If you have learnt any relaxation exercises or breathing techniques, try them now.

The Judges will be listening to your singing carefully. You may be allowed to sing your song all the way through. On the other hand, you may be stopped halfway. You may even be asked to sing something different.

If you are asked to sing a different song, try to stay focused and calm. It's a good sign – it means that the Judges are keen to hear more of your voice. You should have memorised your song choices, so tell them what else you have prepared and allow them to choose from your list.

Natasha Paton

Lloyd Daniels
Series 6

AUDITION DOS AND DON'TS

- Do get a good night's sleep the night before the audition.

- Don't eat anything too heavy just before you audition.

- Do know your songs.

- Don't spend hours singing before your audition.

- Do have backing tracks in the right key for your voice.

- Don't wave your arms around or try to get the audience to sing along with you. This is your audition and they are the fifth Judge, so you have to prove yourself to them too.

- Do believe in yourself. If you don't, no one else will.

- Don't answer back if you don't agree with the Judges.

- Do make up your mind to enjoy the experience.

"This is your BIG, BIG CHANCE."

Louis

Michael Lewis

Raquel Thomas

182700

41

THE AFTERMATH

When you have finished your audition, the Judges have to decide whether you are ready to go on to Bootcamp. In some ways, this is the most stressful moment of the entire audition process.

Your future is hanging in the balance. You're bound to be nervous, but try to stay calm and listen to what the Judges say. It's important!

LISTENING

When you have finished your audition, listen to what the Judges thought of your performance. They have been doing this for a very long time and they certainly know what they are talking about.

It's fine to ask questions, but wait until they have finished speaking. You should aim to get as much feedback as possible. If they praise you, listen closely to what they like about you and your performance.

Treyc Cohen

TAKING CRITICISM

Everyone likes hearing praise. But no singer is perfect, and the best artists are always striving to develop their skills and grow as a performer. The Judges are very experienced, and they may have some negative things to say about your singing voice.

When the Judges are critical, try to listen rather than getting upset or angry. Think of every piece of criticism you get as a tool. You can use it to become a better singer and performer.

In some ways, constructive criticism is better than praise. It shows that the Judges think you can achieve more with your voice, and it gives you an idea of the areas that need work.

Rebecca Ferguson

Jordan Williams

Charlene Dawson

IF IT'S A NO

- Don't beg for another chance. The Judges have made up their minds, and you will only annoy them if you won't take no for an answer.

- Show good grace and manners, and don't lose your temper.

- Smile and thank the Judges before you walk off the stage.

- As soon as you can, write down everything that the Judges said. It's amazing how quickly you will forget their words. Even a few hours later your memory may fail you.

- Use your notes in the following days and months to identify the areas you need to work on.

- Come back next year and try again at the auditions.

IF IT'S A YES

Don't relax for a moment, because the longer you stay in the competition, the harder it's going to get. If you make it to the live shows, stay focused. The real competition has only just begun!

- Don't let shyness stop you from chatting to fans.

- Try to keep cool, even if you feel stressed.

- Remember that the cameras will be watching you all the time, so be yourself.

- Never stop working on improving your singing skills.

- Be glad of all constructive criticism you receive.

- Stay focused on your career.

- Identify an interest that will take your mind off the pressures of stardom – reading or learning to play an instrument, for example.

THE AUDITIONS

This year, millions of fans have tuned in to watch *The X Factor* in living rooms up and down the country. But what is it like for those lucky people who are actually there in person?

THE AUDIENCE

In each city, thousands of people queue up for hours to get into the *X Factor* audience. They are all hoping to see their favourite Judge and to witness some truly spectacular performances. Not everyone is fortunate enough to get into the auditorium, but the lucky few eagerly take their seats and wait for the show to begin.

There's a tangible sense of excitement in the air. Whoops and squeals fill the auditorium, and friends chatter to each other, anticipating the fun ahead. The members of the audience are in a very privileged position. They will see more of the auditions than there is time to show on TV, and they will also hear more of what the Judges have to say.

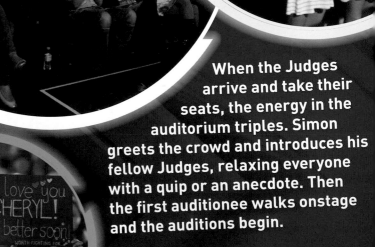

When the Judges arrive and take their seats, the energy in the auditorium triples. Simon greets the crowd and introduces his fellow Judges, relaxing everyone with a quip or an anecdote. Then the first auditionee walks onstage and the auditions begin.

Fans in the crowd hold up banners with messages for the Judges. Audience members call out advice and opinions, and throw themselves into the role of Judge with huge enthusiasm. By the time the auditions have reached an end, the audience has played a vital part in making dreams come true.

Auditorium
Auditions
Upstairs

THE AUDITIONEES

Backstage, the auditionees are excited and terrified at the same time. There is enormous pressure on their shoulders. To walk into the spotlight and face an audience of thousands is daunting for the most confident performer. For those whose nerves are jangling, it's overwhelming.

For many, this is the most important moment in their life so far, and they intend to make the most of it. As the auditionee waits to perform for the Judges, a million thoughts are jostling for attention. Will a smile light up Cheryl's face? Will Louis bounce up and down in his seat with excitement? Will Simon nod in impressed approval?

The reaction of the audience is equally as important as the reaction of the Judges. The audience represents the people who may vote for the auditionee, and eventually buy his or her albums. To sense that the audience approves gives a performer a swell of pride and happiness.

While one auditionee is onstage singing, the next is waiting in the wings. He or she chats to Dermot and takes the microphone. Then the countdown begins to the moment of truth. It's time to face the future!

HELLO LONDON

It's the middle of summer, the sun is shining and the auditions have moved to the capital city.

Thousands of people have turned up, hoping to be one of the lucky audience members. There's a fantastic energy in the crowd. Suddenly a whirring noise makes everyone look up. There are screams of amazement and cheers as the Judges descend from the sky in a helicopter!

Inside the auditorium, Dermot bounds onstage to say hello to the audience. Three girls dart up to the front to have their photos taken. Then the cameras start rolling and the first act walks nervously onstage.

Its time to face the Judges!

FAST FACTS

London was the first city in the world to have an underground railway.

The River Thames flows through London.

London is the seat of central government in Britain.

London Heathrow is the world's busiest airport.

The entertainment district is known as the West End.

Ruth-Ann St Luce

Age: 16   Song: Will You Still Love Me Tomorrow

Student Ruth-Ann amazes the Judges with her big voice. Her performance has the audience whooping and cheering.

SIMON: YES
LOUIS: YES
CHERYL: YES

RESULT: Ruth-Ann heads to Bootcamp with three yesses.

You were HITTING NOTES I don't think I've ever heard.

"The next couple of hours could change someone's life FOREVER!"

"I'm not sure there's anything UNIQUE about you."

Luke & Samantha

Joseph Apostol

"You came out like a RAPPING BULLDOZER."

Trendee X

Age: 45 & 31   Song: No Regrets

Both girls dream of singing in front of huge audiences. Jenny starts to sing and then Vanessa turns the traditional tune into a rap. They're a hit!

SIMON: YES   LOUIS: YES   CHERYL: YES

RESULT: Their dreams may still come true!

James Platt

Age: 20
Song: Me & Mrs Jones

James is a roofer but he hopes that one day his voice will earn him a living. He has an unusual, slightly nasal tone to his voice and the audience like him, but the Judges are divided.

SIMON: NO
LOUIS: YES
CHERYL: YES

RESULT: James is asked to attend Bootcamp.

"It was CHEESY but it was FUN."

Seven

Age: 21 - 25 Song: Just Dance

SIMON: YES LOUIS: YES CHERYL: YES
RESULT: They are all going to Bootcamp.

The group pours energy into their performance, hoping that their love of music will shine through. The audience cheers and applauds as they wait to hear what the Judges have to say.

Elvis Assadi

Mary Swift

HELLO LONDON

"Come back believing you're a WINNER."

Claudia Smith

Age: 20
Song: Nothing Compares 2 U

Claudia has been singing since she was six. She's a powerful singer and the audience erupts, but the Judges are concerned that she doesn't have enough self-belief.

SIMON: YES	RESULT: Claudia will go on to Bootcamp.
LOUIS: YES	
CHERYL: YES	

Eric Coco

Age: 25
Song: I Want You Back

Eric moved to London dreaming of being a pop star, with just £50 in his pocket. Now he works in a clothes shop, but his dreams haven't changed. Could his audition be the moment that turns his dreams into reality?

SIMON: NO
LOUIS: NO
CHERYL: NO

RESULT: Eric will have to carry on dreaming.

"It was a TOTAL MESS."

Adam Bernard

Amy Lynch

Cyril Grant

Elesha Moses

The Souls

Age: 18   Song: Dance With My Father

Anastasia and Leonard hope that their audition will lead them to worldwide fame. Singing the song that was so successful for Joe McElderry last year, will they be equally as impressive?

SIMON: NO   LOUIS: NO   CHERYL: NO

RESULT: The Souls go home without an invitation to Bootcamp.

"You definitely need to WORK MORE on your harmonies."

Michael Lewis

Age: 26   **Song: Rock With You**

SIMON: NO   **LOUIS: NO**   **CHERYL: NO**

RESULT: He returns to his retail job disappointed.

Michael wants to share his passion for music with the world, inspired by his idol, Michael Jackson. He hopes that his singing will spread love, magic and positivity.

"There was not a **SINGLE NOTE** in tune."

"That was **HIDEOUS!**"

Chris Blackwood

Age: 19   **Song: The Climb**

Chris is a big Cheryl Cole fan, and has even brought along a present for her. The fact that the Judges don't like his singing doesn't bother him – he's met Cheryl, so to him, his day is a big success.

SIMON: NO   **LOUIS: NO**   **CHERYL: NO**

RESULT: The audition fails, but Cheryl is pleased with her present.

J'ham

Katie Waissel

Richard Pomerance

"It was a **BRAVE** thing to do."

Jeffery Lawerence

Adrian Bumbescu

Age: 24   **Song: Fight For This Love**

Adrian models for a living, but his ambition is to become a famous recording artist. It soon becomes clear that he's better at modelling than he is at singing.

SIMON: NO
LOUIS: NO
CHERYL: NO

RESULT: Adrian has to go back to the day job.

HELLO MANCHESTER

A vast crowd has gathered in Manchester to see the Judges and support their friends and family. Guest Judge and American pop princess Nicole Scherzinger arrives first. The crowd cheers as she waves, smiles and signs autographs.

Louis soon follows, and then a scream of excitement announces that Simon has arrived. Cheryl is in hospital with malaria, and the auditions won't be the same without her. But the other Judges are determined that the show must go on.

As soon as everyone is seated, Dermot O'Leary bounds onstage and says hello to the crowd. Then the Judges enter, silhouetted against the lights, and the audience screams in anticipation. The Manchester auditions are officially underway!

FAST FACTS

Manchester became an important industrial city thanks to the textile industry.

The first modern computer was developed in Manchester.

Manchester has produced many leading indie, folk and pop music artists, including Oasis and Take That.

The settlement of Manchester goes back as far as Roman times.

Over twenty Nobel Prize winners have come from Manchester.

Charlene Dawson

Age: 17   Song: Listen

Charlene first auditioned for the show when she was fourteen. She pours emotion and energy into her performance, and then bursts into tears but the Judges are quick to comfort her.

SIMON: YES
LOUIS: YES
NICOLE: YES

RESULT: Charlene is pleased to have three yesses.

"You really put YOUR HEART into it."

Aiden Grimshaw

"There's **NO CHEMISTRY** between you."

"The pig was a little **DISTRACTING.**"

Amy Lousie Aldred

EX!

Age: 52 & 43   Song: Something Stupid

Despite being divorced, Stan and Bebe still sing together and are hoping that *The X Factor* will turn their fortunes around. They believe that they could be as successful as The Beatles or Blondie.

SIMON: NO   LOUIS: NO   NICOLE: NO

RESULT: A disappointing result for EX!

Josh Moore

Age: 24   Song: I Wish

Josh has brought along his childhood keepsake, Piggy, who is stuffed into his trousers. He has lots of energy and fun, and people like him, but is he a potential superstar?

SIMON: NO   LOUIS: NO   NICOLE: NO

RESULT: Josh & Piggy are disappointed.

Damien Devine

"You have an **UNEXPECTED FIRE.**"

Tobias Sumpton

Age: 20   Song: Your Song

SIMON: NO   LOUIS: YES   NICOLE: YES
RESULT: Tobias is through to Bootcamp.

Tobias is looking to the music industry for a change of direction. He sings without a backing track and has a great voice, but it's his attitude to hard work and commitment that worries Simon.

Indigo Rose

Age: 17 - 24
Song: Put Your Loving Hand Out /
I Don't Want To Fall In Love

Rebecca, Amy, Kimberley, Michaela and Mica would like to be as famous as the Pussycat Dolls and Girls Aloud. 'I thought you sounded beautiful,' says Nicole. 'There's something quirky about you.'

SIMON: NO   LOUIS: YES   NICOLE: YES

RESULT: Screams of delight can be heard from backstage as the girls get through.

"To be successful now you've got to be like **WILDCATS!**"

Carole Evans

Callum Strettam

Dean Mychjluk

Section 2

Rachel Chu

Age: 44
Song: Lovin' You

Beauty therapist Rachel is hoping to change her life with a yes from the Judges. However, her nerves get the better of her and Simon bursts into spontaneous laughter and Louis collapses forward onto the desk.

SIMON: NO
LOUIS: NO
NICOLE: NO

RESULT: Rachel takes their reaction well .

"We **LIKE YOU**, we just don't like your singing."

"It was a **GOOD AUDITION.**"

Jamie Tinkler

Age: 29   **Song:** With or Without You

SIMON: NO   LOUIS: YES   NICOLE: YES

RESULT: Jamie is through to Bootcamp.

Since being on the show three years ago, Jamie has learned a lot and is more confident as a performer. He thinks there is a niche for something with a rock edge. Louis and Nicole are impressed, but Simon is not.

"There's no CHEMISTRY."

Sistermatic

Age: 23 & 29   **Song: No More Tears**

Helen and Emma are close sisters who hope to take their love of singing to another level. The audience loves them and is soon cheering and clapping along. 'I was surprised how well you sang,' says Simon.

SIMON: YES   **LOUIS: NO**   **NICOLE: YES**

RESULT: Sistermatic go through but are told to work on their image.

Hazel Jackson

Age: 69
Song: Simply the Best

Hazel decided to apply to *The X Factor* to boost her confidence. The audience adores her and everyone is cheering her on. 'I love you and I like your attitude,' says Simon. 'But nobody could listen to an album of you doing that.'

SIMON: NO
LOUIS: NO
NICOLE: YES

RESULT: It's a no for Hazel. 'But I guarantee after this audition you will have them queuing at the door,' says Simon.

"I love the ENERGY and SPIRIT that you brought to that song."

Gary Bird

Pierre Lafayette-Marsh

Wojciech Piegat

The Mechanics

Candy Rose

Age: 24 - 26
Song: When I Grow Up / Is This Love

Chantella, Manasseh and Marsha look fabulous and have bags of energy, attitude and confidence. They take command of the song, but their singing doesn't match up to their image.

SIMON: NO   **LOUIS: NO**   **NICOLE: NO**

RESULT: Candy Rose have more work to do on their vocals.

"Everything was good OTHER THAN the singing."

HELLO BIRMINGHAM

The X Factor has arrived at the biggest venue in the UK – the NEC in Birmingham. As the audience files in and the music begins to play, the excited chatter of the audience builds to a roar. Will they see one of the final twelve today? Who is the guest Judge? What sort of mood is Simon in?

Impatiently the audience claps faster and faster, trying to bring the Judges out. Someone in the crowd starts a Mexican wave that spreads around the arena, accompanied by shrieks of laughter.

Keri Arrindell

At last the Judges arrive in the auditorium and say hello to the audience. With a fresh city full of talent and Natalie Imbruglia as the guest Judge, everyone is keen to get the auditions started.

FAST FACTS

People from Birmingham are known as 'Brummies'.

Birmingham has officially been a city since 1889.

There is evidence of people living in Birmingham up to 10,400 years ago.

Centenary Square is made up of over half a million hand-laid bricks.

Birmingham's 'Spaghetti Junction' is one of the biggest motorway junctions in Europe.

Patti Eleode

Age: 41
Song: For Your Eyes Only

Patti has been singing since she was young but although she is out of tune, the audience and the Judges warm to her personality and appreciate her enthusiasm.

SIMON: NO **LOUIS: YES**
CHERYL: NO **NATALIE: NO**

RESULT: Patti doesn't make it through to Bootcamp.

"People LIKE YOU."

Matt Raymond-Baker

Phil Duncane

"It's a NO!"

Vicky Jackson

Age: 28   Song: Live And Let Die

Vicky is a tribute singer who hopes to find fame using her own voice. There are whoops and cheers from the audience as she hits the high notes.

SIMON: **YES**   LOUIS: **YES**
CHERYL: **YES**   NATALIE: **YES**

RESULT: As the Judges praise her, Vicky's face lights up with a mixture of relief, excitement and pride.

"You're far TOO GOOD to be a tribute singer."

High Street Boys

Age: 18-21   Song: I Want It That Way

The boys dream of stardom, but their audition doesn't impress the Judges.

SIMON: **NO**   LOUIS: **NO**
CHERYL: **NO**   NATALIE: **NO**

RESULT: The boys have a lot more practising to do before they can prove that they have the 'x factor'.

Nu Status

Age: 19 - 22   Song: Down

There are some familiar faces in this group from 2009 and they are determined to prove that they have what it takes. The audience is on its feet as soon as they start singing.

SIMON: **YES**   LOUIS: **YES**
CHERYL: **YES**   NATALIE: **YES**

RESULT: Nu Status sails through to Bootcamp.

You've kind of done a BRITISH *GLEE*."

HELLO BIRMINGHAM

Ablisa

Age: 17 & 18
Song: That's My Goal

Best friends Abbey and Lisa want to live the dream, but their attitude antagonises the audience, who start booing...

SIMON: NO
LOUIS: NO
CHERYL: NO
NATALIE: NO

RESULT: The girls leave with four nos. It's the end of their audition, their singing career – and their friendship!

"SHUT UP!" Lisa tells the crowd.

Abbey loses her temper and lashes out at Lisa. **"SHE PUNCHED HER IN THE FACE!"** Cheryl gasps.

81231

81230

Abbey storms offstage, followed by her friend. **"ARE THEY COMING BACK?"** asks Simon.

They return but their singing is out of tune.

"WHO ARE YOU?" Lisa asks guest Judge Natalie belligerently.

Chad Kennedy

Age: 19   **Song:** Last

SIMON: NO   **LOUIS: NO**
CHERYL: NO   **NATALIE: NO**

RESULT: Chad goes home without a single yes.

Student Chad wants to be the Michael Bublé of Birmingham, but the Judges are not impressed when they see him reading the lyrics from a piece of paper.

81033

"NOT TODAY thanks."

Brenda Morris

Age: 67   **Song:** So What

Brenda throws herself into her audition with great spirit, a blonde wig and stunning long boots. But is she really what the Judges are looking for?

SIMON: NO   **LOUIS: NO**
CHERYL: NO   **NATALIE: NO**

RESULT: Brenda goes home feeling very disappointed.

61512

"Your voice IS NOT strong enough."

"It WASN'T GREAT."

Karl Reid

Age: 26
Song: The Man Who Can't Be Moved / Ordinary People

The audience likes Karl straight away and claps along as he sings. Even Simon's smiling! 'You've got a beautiful tone to your voice,' says Natalie.

SIMON: YES   LOUIS: YES
CHERYL: YES   NATALIE: YES

RESULT: The Judges feel that Karl has great potential.

"You've got a very SOULFUL VOICE."

Scott Archer

Age: 19   Song: Your Song

Scott would like to be the next Elton John and has performed at family funerals. He is hoping that his audition will impress the Judges.

SIMON: NO   LOUIS: NO
CHERYL: NO   NATALIE: NO

RESULT: The Judges don't think that Scott's voice is strong enough.

Jade Thirlwall

Craig Seeney

"Be ORIGINAL!"

I Candy

Age: 19 - 20   Song: Please Don't Stop the Music

SIMON: YES   LOUIS: YES   CHERYL: YES   NATALIE: NO

RESULT: The girls get a second chance.

Suzanne, Natalie, Sara, Laura and Danielle have been together as a group for twelve months. But the Judges question their chemistry and ask them to get rid of the weak links in the group.

HELLO CARDIFF

Clare Lewis

It's a hot day in Cardiff and people have been queuing for hours, but spirits are high and massive cheers go up as the Judges arrive. In 2009, two of the finalists were discovered in Cardiff. Everyone is looking forward to seeing what talent Wales can produce this year.

The audience files in and audience managers make sure that every chair is filled. Then the lights go down and the excited crowd screams in delight. Through a swirl of smoke and an explosion of dazzling lights, the Judges stride to their desk. With them is guest Judge Pixie Lott, who smiles and waves at the crowd. It's time to start the auditions!

FAST FACTS

Cardiff is the largest city in Wales.

It was given city status in 1905.

Cardiff is built on marshland, on a bed of Triassic stones.

Many episodes of Doctor Who are filmed in and around Cardiff.

Cardiff has hosted many sporting events such as the Six Nations, the FA Cup and the Wales Rally GB.

Kash Dholliwar

Age: 21 Song: Closer

Kash has a strong social conscience and wants to make music in order to give financial help to his favourite charities Everyone is hoping that he'll be great! However, his singing is out of tune and out of time with the music.

SIMON: NO   LOUIS: NO
CHERYL: NO   PIXIE: NO

RESULT: The Judges suggest that Kash goes back to modelling to raise money for charity.

107959

"You sound like you've got a really BAD COLD."

Bada Badoo

Age: 20   Song: I Who Have Nothing

Bada strides onstage with a unique look and it's clear that the audience doesn't quite know what to make of him. However, as soon as he starts to sing, the auditorium erupts. He's brilliant!

SIMON: YES   **LOUIS: YES**
CHERYL: YES   **PIXIE: YES**

RESULT: He's on his way to Bootcamp with four massive yesses.

"That's why we **COME BACK** to Wales every year!"

"You did it **BEAUTIFULLY.**"

Alexandra Sherry

Boden 'Flex' Smith

Kelly Browning

Katie Smith

Age: 18   Song: Use Somebody

SIMON: YES   **LOUIS: YES**
CHERYL: YES   **PIXIE: YES**

RESULT: The Judges are very impressed by Katie's talent.

If Katie can't make it as a pop star she wants to be a drama teacher, but she owes it to herself to try to make her dreams come true first. 'Imagine Louis in a bra,' says Simon, trying to relieve her nerves.

Fiona Robertson

Danomic

Age: 17   Song: Everybody in Love

Daniel and Dominic are looking for a job, but the Judges are not convinced that their future is in the music industry. 'That was probably the most boring audition I've ever heard in my life,' says Simon.

SIMON: NO   **LOUIS: NO**
CHERYL: NO   **PIXIE: NO**

RESULT: Danomic will not be going to Bootcamp.

"Not an ounce of **EMOTION.**"

Gareth Sansom

James England

Age: 21
Song: Stuck in the Middle With You / Hometown Glory

The Judges aren't sure about James's first song, and ask him to sing something different. 'It was much, much better,' says Simon. But he goes on to question James's lack of confidence.

....

SIMON: YES   **LOUIS: NO**
CHERYL: YES   **PIXIE: YES**

....

RESULT: James goes through but he needs more confidence.

"You've got a **GREAT VOICE.**"

"You do have a **REALLY GOOD VOICE.**"

Steven Twimbru

Jamie Lock

Lauren Bennett

Age: 19   Song: Somebody To Love / Mama Do

Lauren is on a gap year and is hoping that her love of music will lead her to new adventures. Simon smiles as she puts her heart and soul into her performance.

....

SIMON: YES   LOUIS: YES   CHERYL: YES   PIXIE: YES

....

RESULT: Lauren is heading for Bootcamp!

"Genuinely, Natasha, you **CAN'T SING.**"

Natasha Paton

Age: 22   Song: Hero / Bleeding Love

SIMON: NO   LOUIS: NO   CHERYL: NO   PIXIE: NO

RESULT: Despite having an *X Factor* tattoo and over 2000 fans on Facebook, it's a no for Natasha.

Natasha tells the Judges that in ten years she'll be bigger and better than Alicia Keys, Natasha starts to sing. Her voice wobbles and she's out of time with the music. 'You can't sing a note,' says Louis.

Rob Burn

Diana Zavina

Age: 37
Song: I'm Coming Out

Although her voice isn't the best, her fun-loving personality endears her to the audience and the Judges. 'I was entertained,' says Cheryl.

SIMON: NO   **LOUIS:** NO
CHERYL: NO   **PIXIE:** NO

RESULT: Diana gets four nos, but she has enjoyed her time on the show.

"You're a **NIPPY LITTLE THING,** aren't you!"

/6062

Lauren Francis

Age: 18   **Song:** Sweet Child of Mine / Heard It Through the Grapevine

Lauren sings in pubs and clubs around Plymouth every weekend but has her feisty, positive attitude shown she's got take her to the live shows?

SIMON: YES   **LOUIS:** YES   **CHERYL:** YES   **PIXIE:** YES

RESULT: Lauren is delighted to be through to the next stage of the competition.

Vivian Hole

Tania Evans

Mierous Hennessy

Christian Lewis

Age: 30   **Song:** Chasing Cars

Full-time dad Christian used to be in the parachute regiment before working as a personal trainer, but now he's hoping that his voice will open up new opportunities.

SIMON: NO   **LOUIS:** NO   **CHERYL:** NO   **PIXIE:** NO

RESULT: It's a no, but Christian is advised to get some experience and then try again next year.

"Your **NERVES** really showed through your vocals."

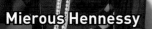

Myles Blair

HELLO DUBLIN

The X Factor has arrived in Ireland's capital, and Louis Walsh is brimming with excitement. He's hoping that there will be plenty of talent waiting to be discovered in his home country.

As the audience hurries to fill the seats, the atmosphere is charged with anticipation. It is four years since the show visited Ireland, and the Judges have high expectations.

Katy Perry is the guest Judge, and she cannot wait to throw herself into her new role. She takes time to greet the audience before sitting down to await the first auditionee. Like the other Judges and the audience, she is hoping to spot a diamond in the rough.

FAST FACTS

Dublin was founded as a Viking settlement.

The city has produced some of the greatest writers of all time, including W.B. Yeats, Samuel Beckett and Oscar Wilde.

Dublin has been named a UNESCO City of Literature.

Guinness is brewed in Dublin.

Dublin is twinned with Barcelona.

Stephen Concannon

Age: 23   Song: Your Song

Beach lifeguard Stephen not only serenades Cheryl – he even runs offstage to get closer to her and hold her hand. Simon isn't impressed, but the other Judges are as delighted as the audience.

SIMON: NO   **LOUIS: YES**
CHERYL: YES   **KATY: YES**

RESULT: Stephen heads to Bootcamp with three yesses.

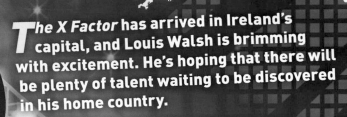

"The vocals were TERRIBLE."

Temple Fire

Age: 20 - 22 Song: Wake Me Up

This local boy band have been friends for about ten years. They want to set the venue alight with the intensity of their singing and dancing and the boys rehearse up to six hours per day. They certainly talk the talk, but can they walk the walk?.

SIMON: NO LOUIS: NO
CHERYL: NO KATY: NO

RESULT: There is more rehearsing needed before next year's auditions.

"That was NOT SERIOUS, was it?"

Alex Skyes

Tyrone Murphy

"I'm SPEECHLESS."

Underground

Rebecca Creighton

Sadbh O'Donnell

Age: 18 Song: Beautiful Disaster

Part-time waitress Sadbh is from the west of Ireland. She impresses three of the Judges with her soft, melodic voice, but one Judge is hard to please. 'I don't see any personality,' Simon remarks.

SIMON: NO LOUIS: YES CHERYL: YES KATY: YES

RESULT: Sadbh is through to the next stage, but without a yes from Simon.

"You've got a GORGEOUS VOICE."

HELLO DUBLIN

Mary Byrne

"I think you've GOT POTENTIAL."

Emma Barry

Sugar Bullet

Age: 17 - 21   Song: The Scientist

SIMON: NO   LOUIS: YES
CHERYL: YES   KATY: YES

RESULT: The girls are delighted to be through to the next stage of the competition.

This five-piece girl group walk onstage looking eager to get on with their audition. They perform without a backing track, and it's obvious that their harmonies have been carefully worked out and practised. The audience likes them, but not all the Judges agree.

"I've just got a BAD FEELING."

Carl Gibney

Barbara Allen

"You are absolutely ADORABLE."

Dwayne Edgar

Age: 16
Song: Don't Stop Believin'

Dwayne wants to be just like Robbie Williams and he doesn't disappoint! The audience is soon on its feet, and he even has Katy Perry singing along. The crowd clearly adores him, and the Judges are impressed.

SIMON: NO   LOUIS: YES
CHERYL: YES   KATY: YES

RESULT: Dwayne is overjoyed to be going to Bootcamp.

"You've got a lot of CHARM."

Fadil Bara

Nial Horan

Ben Dillon

235431

Lode Vermeulen

Age: 35
Song: The Tiger Song

Lode walks confidently out onstage to the astonishment and bewilderment of all four Judges. His big pussycat growls and sense of fun do not impress Simon. 'I thought he was OK,' says Louis with a shrug.

SIMON: NO	**LOUIS: NO**
CHERYL: NO	**KATY: NO**

RESULT: Lode leaves with empty paws.

"NO, NO, NO!"

Eddie Kenny

Age: 46
Song: Livin' On a Prayer

Eddie enjoys putting passion and emotion into his performances. He describes himself as a 'heavy metal maniac'. He pours energy and enthusiasm into his performance, but his singing is cut short by Simon.

SIMON: NO	**LOUIS: NO**
CHERYL: NO	**KATY: NO**

RESULT: No yesses for Eddie, despite his passion.

"You gave it a go but it's a NO."

Double D

246063

Sean & Robbie

65

HELLO GLASGOW

It's a big day for the musical talent of Glasgow! The auditions have arrived in Scotland and hopeful singers are gathering backstage. Meanwhile, crowds of fans wait at the entrance to catch a glimpse of their favourite Judges.

Inside, expectations are high. Everyone in the audience is hoping that this year's winner will hail from Scotland. The Judges arrive and take their places. The guest Judge is Geri Halliwell, and she is eager to find new talent.

The auditorium lights dim and the spotlight shines on the first act of the day. Will Scotland produce a good crop of talent this year? There's only one way to find out!

GET WELL CHERY

FAST FACTS

Glasgow is the largest city in Scotland.

St Mungo is Glasgow's patron saint.

Glasgow has its own Poet Laureate.

A tramway system and a subway run through the city.

Glasgow will be the host city of the 2014 Commonwealth Games.

Hollie Burns

Age: 25   Song: Creep

Hollie has been getting experience singing in the pubs and clubs around Glasgow, and now she wants to put her talent to the test. The audience goes crazy with delight. Even the Judges are applauding!

SIMON: YES
LOUIS: YES
CHERYL: YES
GERI: YES

RESULT: Hollie goes on to Bootcamp with all the Judges supporting her.

21257

"You could be a POPSTAR."

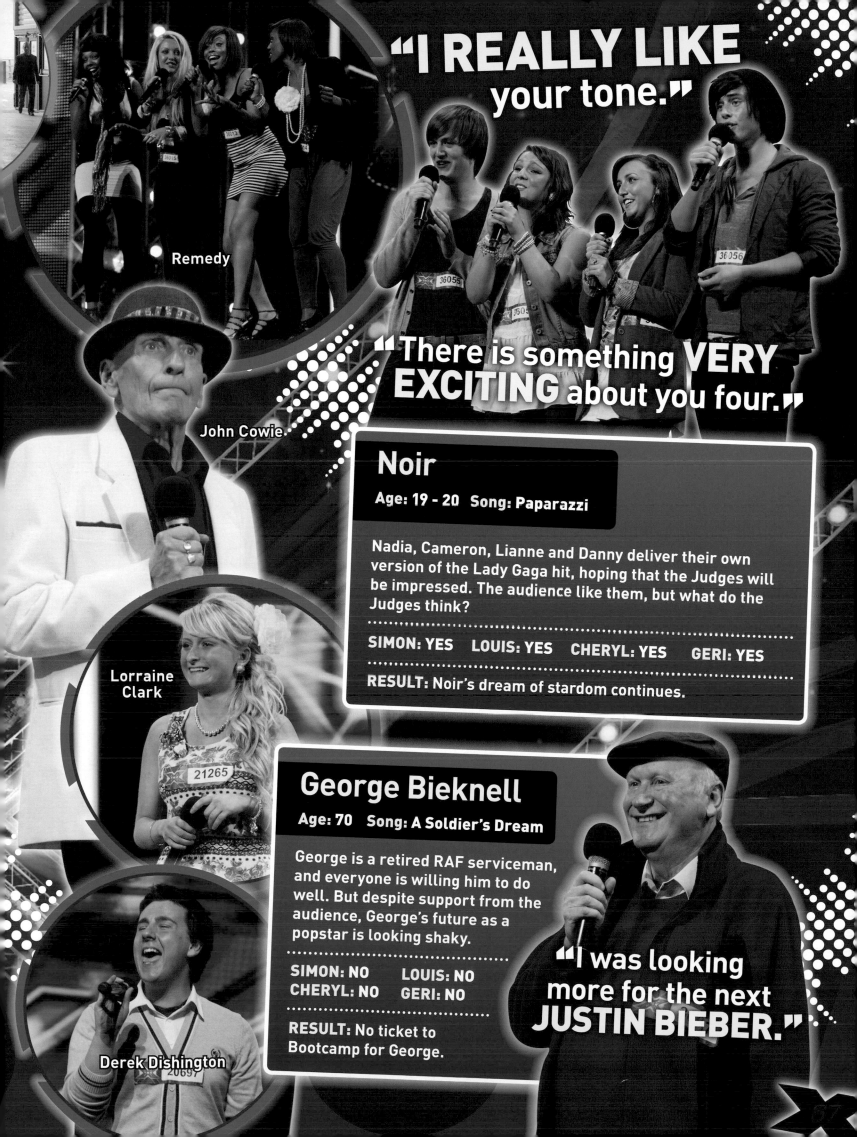

"I REALLY LIKE your tone."

Remedy

There is something VERY EXCITING about you four.

John Cowie

Noir

Age: 19 - 20   Song: Paparazzi

Nadia, Cameron, Lianne and Danny deliver their own version of the Lady Gaga hit, hoping that the Judges will be impressed. The audience like them, but what do the Judges think?

SIMON: YES   LOUIS: YES   CHERYL: YES   GERI: YES

RESULT: Noir's dream of stardom continues.

Lorraine Clark

George Bieknell

Age: 70   Song: A Soldier's Dream

George is a retired RAF serviceman, and everyone is willing him to do well. But despite support from the audience, George's future as a popstar is looking shaky.

SIMON: NO   LOUIS: NO
CHERYL: NO   GERI: NO

RESULT: No ticket to Bootcamp for George.

"I was looking more for the next JUSTIN BIEBER."

Derek Dishington

HELLO GLASGOW

G & S

Age: 37 & 21
Song: Don't Stop Believin' / Get Here

Peter and Caroline are good friends and have worked up the courage to audition together, but the Judges want to hear Caroline audition solo. Peter supports Caroline as she stands in the centre of the stage and sings alone.

SIMON: NO **LOUIS: YES**
CHERYL: YES **GERI: YES**

RESULT: Caroline's courage pays off – she's through to Bootcamp!

"I wish I had a FRIEND LIKE HIM."

Naomi Fyfe

Cathy O'Rourke

David Graham

Gamu Nhengu

Mark McGregor

Age: 21
Song: Turn Back the Hands of Time

Support worker Mark is a big hit with the audience, and they wave their hands in the air as he sings. The Judges are equally as impressed. 'This is why we come back to Scotland,' says Simon.

SIMON: YES **LOUIS: YES**
CHERYL: YES **GERI: YES**

RESULT: Mark is through to the next stage of the competition.

"Mark YOU'VE GOT IT!"

Cheryl Ledgerwood

"I think you have a really GOOD VOICE."

Stephen Hunter

Age: 41   Song: Disco Inferno

This year's first auditionee, Stephen captures the imagination of the audience and Judges alike with his larger than life character and dance moves.

SIMON: YES   LOUIS: YES   CHERYL: YES   GERI: YES

RESULT: Stephen kicks the show off with a bang, getting four yeses!

Lynn Frances O'Neil

Age: 23
Song: True Colours

Lynn is a waitress, and she loves singing so much that she can't stop – even when she's serving customers! Her performance delights the Judges and ends the auditions on a high.

SIMON: YES   LOUIS: YES
CHERYL: YES   GERI: YES

RESULT: With four huge yesses, Lynn heads off to Bootcamp.

"If I owned the restaurant I'd have you SINGING EVERY NIGHT of the week."

Garry Greig

"It sounded and looked like YOU JUST MET EACH OTHER at a bus stop."

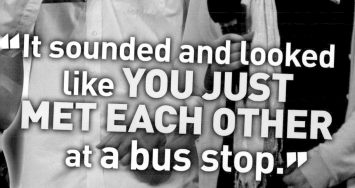

Diva Features

Age: 23   Song: Waiting For a Star To Fall

These three friends dream of performing at the Super Bowl. They launch into their audition with plenty of energy and enthusiasm, but something just isn't working for the hard-to-please Judges.

SIMON: NO   LOUIS: NO   CHERYL: NO   GERI: NO

RESULT: Diva Features go home disappointed.

X FACTOR FACTS

Check out these behind-the-scenes shots and fascinating facts from *The X Factor* 2010.

London officially had the **LOUDEST** audience of all the audition cities.

During the auditions and Bootcamp, **14,980** bottles of water were drunk.

The Judges got through **ten** large bottles of water and **three** limes each day.

The Judges traveled over **1,500** miles searching for the best singers in the country.

A total of **8** different judges have decided who cuts it to Bootcamp (Simon, Louis, Cheryl, Pixie, Natalie, Katy, Nicole and Geri)

The Judges and crew ate **thirty-eight** trolleys of snacks.

A total of **4,945** pens were used by the Judges and crew.

The Judges consumed **490** chocolate bars during the auditions and Bootcamp.

Busy camera operators filmed **896** hours of footage at the auditions.

Across the six audition cities, **72,000** audience members watched the auditionees try to impress the Judges.

BOOTCAMP

Over two hundred people arrived at Bootcamp hoping that their dreams would come true. They had all done well at the audition stage, but now they had to do even better. Choosing the wrong song or forgetting the lyrics could spell the end of their hopes. Who would fall by the wayside, and who would be heading for the Judges' Houses?

This year's Bootcamp was held at Wembley Arena, and there were several changes to the format from last year.

One of the biggest differences was the fact that Dannii and Cheryl were not able to be there. However, there were experts on hand to help Simon and Louis make their decisions. The Judges were joined by vocal coaches, a stylist and music producers from Sony, as well as creative director Brian Friedman.

Nu Status

Before Bootcamp officially started there was group vocal coaching within the categories. Another change to the normal routine was that all contestants had to prove that they had the ability to learn dance moves.

John Adeleye

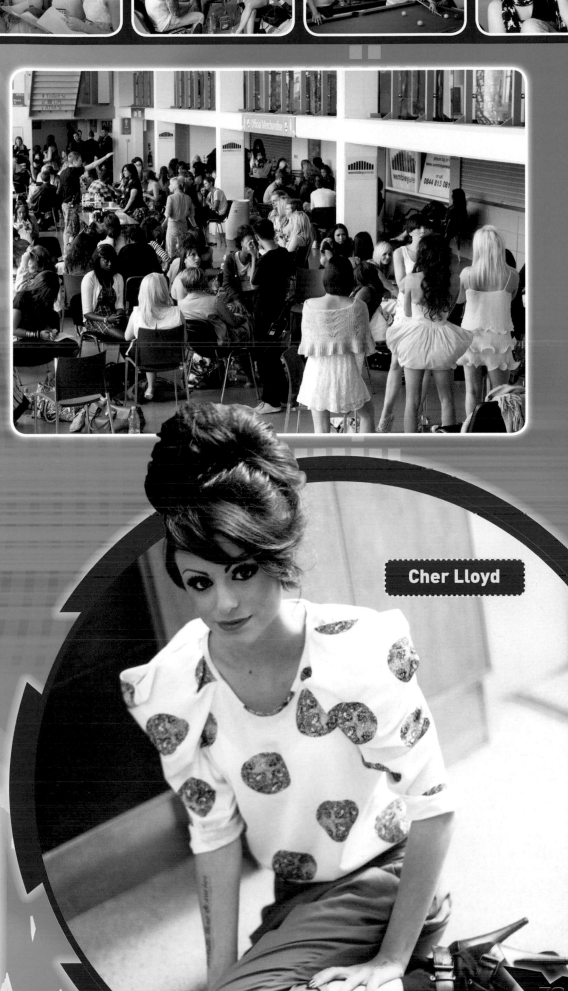

Cher Lloyd

Guest Judge Nicole Scherzinger suggested that the Boys and Girls categories should include anyone under the age of twenty-eight, hoping that this would strengthen the competition.

Because Cheryl and Dannii missed the auditions, it was decided to put eight acts through to each of the Judges' Houses instead of the usual six. This would give them a wider variety of contestants to choose from.

BOOTCAMP SCHEDULE

Day 1:	Category chorus line-ups.
Day 2:	Choreography.
Day 3:	Final performance.

BOOTCAMP

DAY 1

On the first day of Bootcamp, there was one chorus line up per category. Everyone stood in a row and then stepped forward to sing in turn.

GIRLS:
'If I Were a Boy' by Beyoncé

BOYS:
'Man in the Mirror' by Michael Jackson

GROUPS:
'Nothing's Gonna Stop Us Now' by Starship

OVERS:
'Poker Face' by Lady Gaga

The Judges listened carefully, aware that a double responsibility rested on their shoulders. Not only did they have to pick out the cream of Britain's singing talent, they also had to speak on behalf of the two missing Judges, Cheryl and Dannii.

At the end of the first day, one hundred contestants were told that they had reached the end of their *X Factor* journey.

DAY 2

Day two of Bootcamp found the contestants learning a complicated dance routine before performing it onstage with the others in their category. They danced to 'Telephone' by Lady Gaga.

The experts were called in to advise the Judges, but no feedback was given to the contestants.

Husstle

DAY 3

On the final day of Bootcamp, the contestants were asked to pick one song from a given list. Louis and Simon were joined by guest Judge Nicole Scherzinger.

The contestants performed their songs with backing tracks, but there were no comments from the Judges' after the performances.

Bada Budoo

Gamu Nhengu

Adam Bernard

Treyc Cohen

BOOTCAMP SONG LIST

- 'A Song For You' - Donny Hathaway
- 'Ain't No Mountain High Enough' - Diana Ross / Marvin Gaye & Tammi Terrell
- 'Angel of Harlem' - U2
- 'Bad Romance' - Lady Gaga
- 'Born to Run' - Bruce Springsteen
- 'Champagne Supernova' - Oasis
- 'Come Home' - One Republic
- 'Crazy For You' – Madonna
- 'Creep' – Radiohead
- 'Fix You' – Coldplay
- 'Footprints In The Sand' – Leona Lewis
- 'Get It On' – T.Rex
- 'Gravity' – Embrace
- 'Heroes' – David Bowie
- 'I Don't Feel Like Dancing' – Scissor Sisters
- 'I've Got A Feeling' – Black Eyed Peas
- 'Life On Mars' – David Bowie
- 'Like A Star' – Corinne Bailey Rae
- 'Live and Let Die' – Wings
- 'Make You Feel My Love' – Adele
- 'Pack Up' – Eliza Doolittle
- 'Paradise City' – Guns N' Roses
- 'Party In The U.S.A.' – Miley Cyrus
- 'Somewhere Only We Know' – Keane
- 'Shout' – Tears For Fears
- 'Stop Crying Your Heart Out' – Leona Lewis / Oasis
- 'Sweet Child o' Mine' – Guns N' Roses
- 'The First Time Ever I Saw Your Face' – Leona Lewis / Roberta Flack
- 'The Jean Genie' – David Bowie
- 'This Year's Love' – David Gray
- 'Viva La Vida' – Coldplay
- 'Walk On By' – Dionne Warwrick
- 'Walk This Way' – Aerosmith
- 'We Belong Together' – Mariah Carey
- 'What's Going On' – Marvin Gaye
- 'Wishing On A Star' – Rose Royce
- 'Your Song' – Moulin Rouge Soundtrack / Elton John

The contestants had to choose one song from this list.

BOOTCAMP'S BEST

Princes and Rogues hugely impressed Simon at Bootcamp. Singing 'Nothing's Gonna Stop Us Now' and 'Bad Romance', they sizzled with energy onstage. 'There is a place for a band like them,' Simon said.

Princes and Rogues

"People LOVE a bit of camp."
Louis

Diva Fever

"A BIG surprise."
Louis

John Wilding

"He's a PERFORMER."
Simon

Aiden Grimshaw

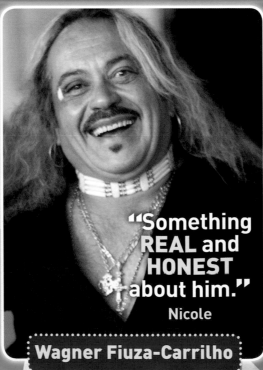

"Something REAL and HONEST about him."
Nicole

Wagner Fiuza-Carrilho

"He's a DIVA."
Simon

Paije Richardson

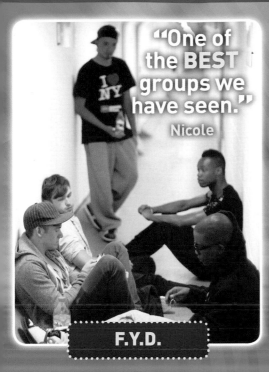

"One of the BEST groups we have seen."
Nicole

F.Y.D.

"He IS worth it."
Louis

Tom Richards

The Reason

"You can throw great songs at them and they will make them MODERN and FUN."
Louis

"Every little DIVA rolled into one."
Louis

Yuli Minguel

"I LIKE him."
Simon

Nicolo Festa

"He has a GREAT style."
Louis

Marlon McKenzie

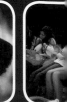

BOOTCAMP

When all the contestants had performed, it was time for the Judges to make their final decisions. They based their choices on the performances they had seen throughout Bootcamp, as well as the opinions of the experts they had called upon.

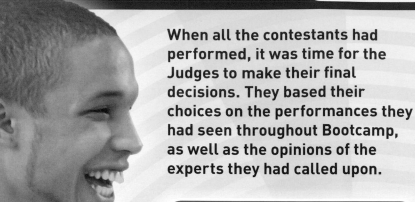

Keri Arrindell

Karl Brown

THROUGH TO THE JUDGES' HOUSES

BOYS
Mentor: Dannii
Aiden Grimshaw
John Wilding
Karl Brown
Marlon McKenzie
Matt Cardle
Nicolo Festa
Paije Richardson
Tom Richards

Raquel Thomas

THROUGH TO THE JUDGES' HOUSES

GIRLS
Mentor: Cheryl
Annastasia Baker
Cher Lloyd
Gamu Nhengu
Katie Waissel
Keri Arrindell
Raquel Thomas
Rebecca Ferguson
Treyc Cohen

Annastasia Baker

THROUGH TO THE JUDGES' HOUSES

OVER 28s
Mentor: Louis

Elesha Moses
John Adeleye
Justin Vanderhyde
Mary Byrne
Stephen Hunter
Storm Lee
Wagner Fiuza-Carrilho
Yuli Minguel

Husstle

Some decisions were easy to make, while others divided the Judges. But after much discussion and debate, the final thirty-two acts were chosen. All that remained was to let the contestants know which of them would be going on to the next stage...

THROUGH TO THE JUDGES' HOUSES

GROUPS
Mentor: Simon

1Direction
Belle Amie
Diva Fever
F.Y.D.
Husstle
Princes and Rogues
The Reason
Twem

Storm Lee

Justin Vanderhyde

Twem

Wagner Fiuza-Carrilho

JUDGES' HOUSES
SIMON ↘

Simon took the Groups to the beautiful beach city of Marbella, Spain, where they would face their biggest challenge to date.

Simon entertained the largest number of contestants, and in Marbella he was able to show them how the rich and famous live. They stayed in a villa that had three pools, a private cinema and a gym, as well as a stunning backdrop of mountains.

Judges' Houses FAST **FACTS**

Location: Marbella

Category: Groups

Guest Mentor: Sinitta

Contestants:
1Direction
Belle Amie
Diva Fever
FYD
Husstle
Princes and Rogues
The Reason
Twem

The Reason
Age: 26 - 29
Home town: London
Job: Electrician, Crane Driver, Painter, Unemployed

"You actually sound VERY GOOD."

The groups experienced a lifestyle that they had only ever imagined. It made them more determined than ever to become successful recording artists. Accompanied by piano and guitar, they sang their hearts out for their mentor.

"A sense of STYLE and believeable."

Simon had Sinitta to help him make a decision, but the choice was agonising. From all the thousands of people who had auditioned, he now had eight to choose from. Who would best represent him in the live shows? Whose dreams were about to come true?

"I LIKE that group."

Husstle
Age: 19 - 29
Home town: Manchester
Job: Student, Dance Teachers, Estate Agent

"You're FUN!"

Diva Fever
Age: 21 & 26
Home town: Manchester
Job: Student, Customer services assistant

GROUPS
SONG LIST

1DIRECTION
'Torn' & 'My Life Would Suck Without You'

BELLE AMIE
'Nothing On You' & 'Faith'

DIVA FEVER
'Strong Enough' & 'Love Machine'

F.Y.D.
'Beggin' & 'Halo' / 'Dangerously In Love'

HUSSTLE
'Mmm Bop' & 'Tainted Love'

PRINCES AND ROGUES
'Relax' & 'Video Killed the Radio Star'

THE REASON
'If Your Not the One' & 'Waterfalls'

TWEM
'When Love Takes Over' & 'Crazy'

MARBELLA LOWDOWN

Marbella sits in a dazzling location on the shores of the Mediterranean, below La Concha mountain. It is a popular destination for wealthy celebrities and features the famous Golden Mile, home to some of the area's most impressive villas.

F.Y.D.

Belle Amie

1Direction

Through to the live shows...

1Direction
F.Y.D.
Belle Amie

JUDGES' HOUSES
LOUIS ↘

Louis took his category, the Overs, to Shannon, Ireland, hoping to inspire their performances with a little Irish charm.

This was the contestants' final chance to reach the live stage of the competition. Over the course of three days, they had to perform to the best of their ability and try to win the admiration of Louis and Sharon Osbourne.

Judges' Houses
FAST FACTS

Location: Shannon

Category: Overs

**Guest Mentor:
Sharon Osbourne**

**Contestants:
Mary Byrne**

Wagner Fiuza-Carrilho

Justin Vanderhyde

John Adeyele

Storm Lee

Stephen Hunter

Elesha Moses

Yuli Minguel

"You bring FUN."

Yuli Minguel

Age: 32

Home town: Manchester

Job: Student coach

It wasn't all hard work. While staying in Ireland, Louis treated the contestants to a clay pigeon shoot to help them relax. However, no one forgot the real reason they were there.

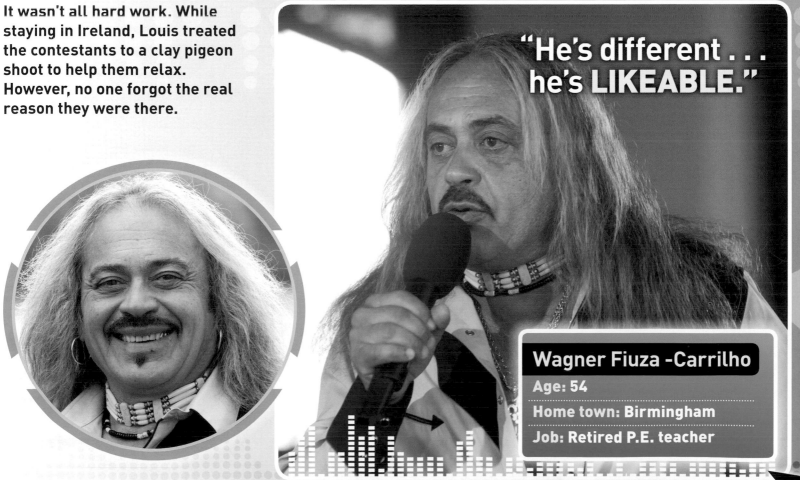

"He's different . . . he's LIKEABLE."

Wagner Fiuza -Carrilho

Age: 54

Home town: Birmingham

Job: Retired P.E. teacher

JUDGES' HOUSES
LOUIS ↘

While they were at the house, each contestant performed two songs. They could choose whether to sing acapella or to be accompanied by a piano. Each of them was fizzing with excitement and anticipation, as well as a lot of nerves. Which of them would be able to take command of those nerves and channel them into their performances?

Elesha Moses
Age: 29
Home town: London
Job: Support worker

"This girl is really, **REALLY GOOD**"

Stephen Hunter
Age: 41
Home town: Lanarkshire
Job: House husband

"An **INTERESTING** Pavarotti."

Justin Vanderhyde
Age: 30
Home town: Birmingham
Job: Entertainer

"You look a bit like an **ACTION FIGURE** man."

OVER 28's SONG LIST

ELESHA MOSES
'Gravity' &
'If I Ain't Got You'

JOHN ADELEYE
'Underneath Your Clothes'
& 'Billionaire'

JUSTIN VANDERHYDE
'Telephone' &
'I Kissed a Girl'

MARY BYRNE
'I Didn't Know My Own
Strength' & 'Fix You'

STEPHEN HUNTER
'Get the Party Started' &
'One Moment in Time'

STORM LEE
'Hot and Cold' &
'Without You'

WAGNER FIUZA-CARRILHO
'You Got the Love'
& 'Hero'

YULI MINGUEL
'Bonkers' &
'Midnight Train to Georgia'

SHANNON **LOWDOWN**

Shannon is an area of stunning scenery, rich history and fascinating attractions. From the grandeur of King John's Castle to the timeless sights of Folk Park, there is plenty to do and discover. Louis chose a beautiful setting that his contestants will never forget.

Through to the live shows...

Storm Lee
John Adeleye
Mary Byrne

JUDGES' HOUSES
CHERYL ↘

Cheryl had missed the Manchester auditions and Bootcamp due to a bout of malaria. However, she recovered in time to take her acts to Ascot, the prestigious home of the Royal Ascot race meeting.

Cheryl's acts arrived at the Ascot house full of excitement and anticipation. It was like a dream come true to reach this stage of the competition. However, now that their goal was so close, the stakes had never been higher.

Judges' Houses
FAST **FACTS**

Location: Ascot

Category: The Girls

Guest Mentor: Will.i.am

Contestants:

Annastasia Baker

Cher Lloyd

Gamu Nhengu

Katie Waissel

Keri Arrindell

Raquel Thomas

Rebecca Ferguson

Treyc Cohen

"It's taken a lot of **COURAGE** and hard work to come back out here."

Annastasia Baker
Age: 21

Home town: London

Job: Full-time Mum

"You are not aware of how **GOOD** you are."

Raquel Thomas

Age: **19**

Home town: **London**

Job: **Student**

Cheryl ensured that the girls had the chance to relax and enjoy their time in Ascot. She gave them as much support and encouragement as she could. But in the end, their destiny lay in her hands, and it was vital to make the correct decision.

"I could **RELY** on you."

Treyc Cohen

Age: **26**

Home town: **Birmingham**

Job: **Claims handler**

JUDGES' HOUSES
CHERYL ↘

On the third day of their visit, the girls waited anxiously to hear who would be representing Cheryl in the live shows. Each girl had her hopes for the future resting on this moment. Who would have their efforts rewarded and who would fall at the last hurdle?

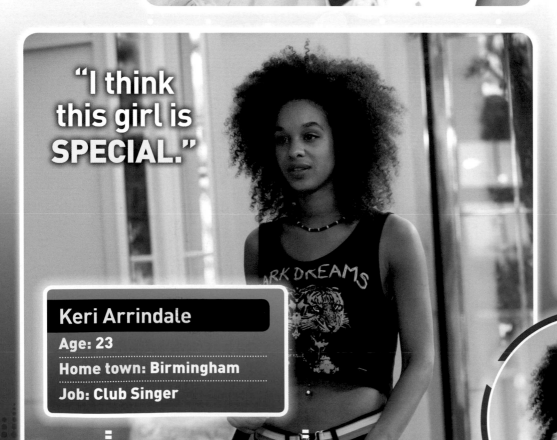

Gamu Nhengu
Age: 18
Home town: Glasgow
Job: Student

"You made me **EXCITED.**"

"I think this girl is **SPECIAL.**"

Keri Arrindale
Age: 23
Home town: Birmingham
Job: Club Singer

THE GIRLS
SONG LIST

ANNASTASIA BAKER
'How Can An Angel Break My Heart' & 'Sweet Dreams'

CHER LLOYD
'Cooler Than Me' & 'Ignition'

GAMU NHENGU
'Don't Know Why' & 'Cry Me Out'

KATIE WAISSEL
'Smile' & 'Save Me From Myself'

KERI ARRINDELL
'Scientist' & 'Wake Me Up When September Ends'

RAQUEL THOMAS
'Just Like A Star' & 'Ordinary People'

REBECCA FERGUSON
'Fireflies' & 'Another Day In Paradise'

TREYC COHEN
'Ave Maria' & 'Show Me Love'

LONDON **LOWDOWN**

Ascot is a small town in Berkshire, and it's famous as the location of Royal Ascot, one of the world's best-known race meetings. The Royal Family attends the meeting in a horse-drawn carriage, and the fashions and famous faces of Ascot are splashed across newspapers and magazines across the world. It's the perfect setting for Cheryl's glamorous final eight to give the performances of their lives.

Through to the live shows...

Katie Waissel
Cher Lloyd
Rebecca Ferguson

JUDGES' HOUSES
DANNII ↘

Dannii flew the boys out to Cairns, where she had a tough decision to make. Which three would she choose as her finalists?

The boys were delighted to discover that Dannii was going to be their mentor. Although she hadn't been able to attend the auditions, she had kept in close contact with the other Judges and knew all about her final eight contestants.

Judges' Houses
FAST **FACTS**

Location: Cairns

Category: The Boys

Guest Mentor:
Natalie Imbruglia

Contestants:

Aiden Grimshaw

Nicolo Festa

Paije Richardson

Marlon McKenzie

John Wilding

Tom Richards

Karl Brown

Matt Cardle

Marlon McKenzie
Age: 27
Home town: Manchester
Job: Receptionist / Model

"He gave it EVERYTHING."

The boys' second day at Dannii's house was devoted to their performances. Accompanied by a piano, each act sang two songs. When everyone had performed, it was Dannii's job to choose the three who would be most likely to do well in the competition.

Karl Brown

Age: **19**

Home town: **Richmond**

Job: **Trainee electrician**

"I think he is WORTH IT."

Tom Richards

Age: **16**

Home town: **Cardiff**

Job: **Student**

JUDGES' HOUSES
DANNII ↘

The boys had a lot of fun in Cairns. Dannii wanted their experience of her home to be unforgettable. But all their deepest hopes were pinned on the last day of their visit – the moment when Dannii would either give them the chance of a lifetime . . . or bring an end to their *X Factor* journey.

"A big SURPRISE."

John Wilding
Age: 17
Home town: London
Job: Student

Paije Richardson
Age: 19
Home town: London
Job: Student

"He is a DIVA."

THE BOYS
SONG LIST

AIDEN GRIMSHAW
'Jealous Guy' &
'Cannon Ball'

JOHN WILDING
'Try Sleeping With A Broken Heart' & 'Back for Good'

KARL BROWN
'Russian Roulette'
& 'She Said'

MARLON MCKENZIE
'By Your Side' &
'Empire State of Mind'

MATT CARDLE
'Come Home' &
'If I Were A Boy'

NICOLO FESTA
'New York' &
'Beautiful'

PAIJE RICHARDSON
'True Colours' &
'Halo'

TOM RICHARDS
'Feel' &
'Carry You Home'

CAIRNS LOWDOWN

The Great Barrier Reef is close to Cairns, which is a city that's very conscious of the natural world around it. Rainforestation Nature Park, Tjapukai Aboriginal Cultural Park and Kuranda Skyrail Rainforest Cableway are all close by. And no one should visit Cairns without experiencing the magnificent swimming lagoon!

Through to the live shows...

Aiden Grimshaw
Matt Cardle
Nicolo Festa

95

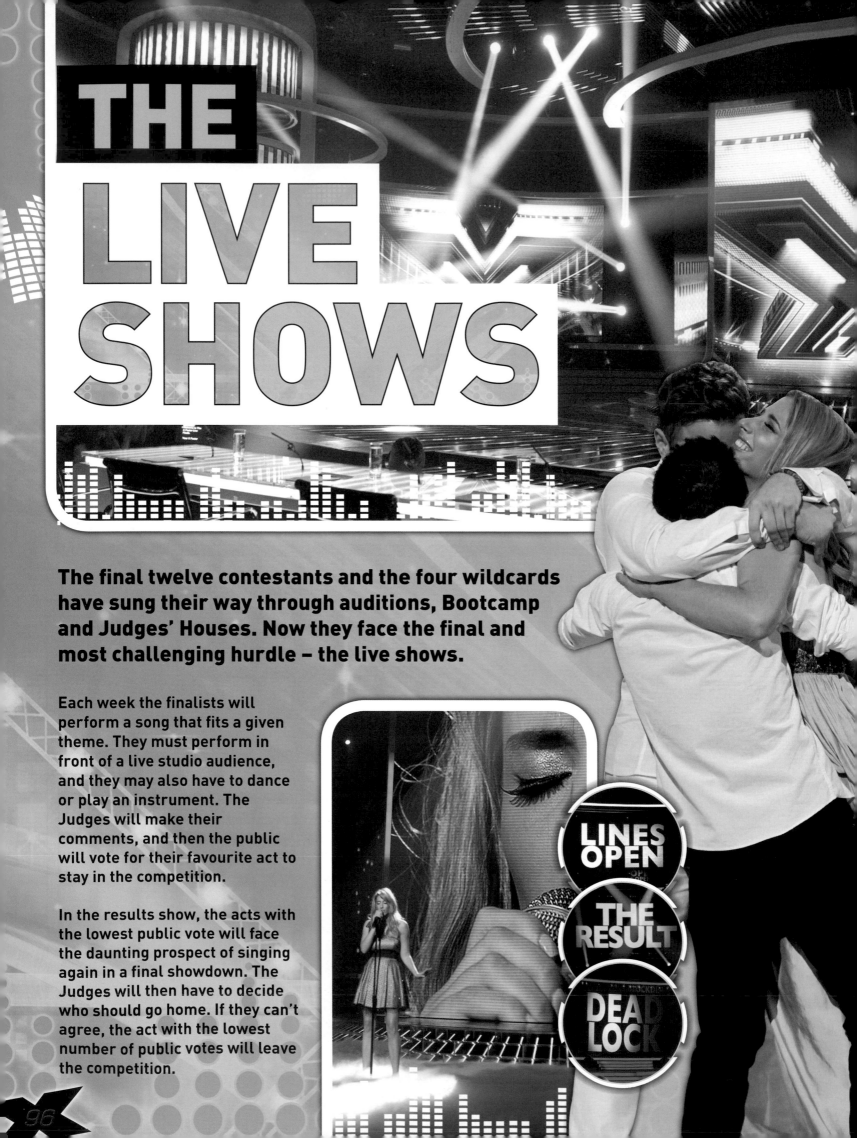

THE LIVE SHOWS

The final twelve contestants and the four wildcards have sung their way through auditions, Bootcamp and Judges' Houses. Now they face the final and most challenging hurdle – the live shows.

Each week the finalists will perform a song that fits a given theme. They must perform in front of a live studio audience, and they may also have to dance or play an instrument. The Judges will make their comments, and then the public will vote for their favourite act to stay in the competition.

In the results show, the acts with the lowest public vote will face the daunting prospect of singing again in a final showdown. The Judges will then have to decide who should go home. If they can't agree, the act with the lowest number of public votes will leave the competition.

LINES OPEN

THE RESULT

DEAD LOCK

As the weeks go by, the number of contestants will dwindle, and the pressure will increase. Nerves, illness and stress can affect their performances, and the dreams can be shattered by just one slip or wrong note.

The format of the show changes when there are five contestants left in the competition. Each finalist sings two songs in the first show, with the public vote opening after the first performance. The act with the fewest public votes will be automatically eliminated from the competition. The Judges will cease to have a vote and their role will be to comment on the performances.

Three acts will go into the grand final, where the winner will be decided by public vote over the course of two live shows. The first show will feature the contestants' performances and explore each one's individual development and *X Factor* experience. The second show will reveal the results of the public vote, and will showcase the winner's debut single.

Guest stars often perform on the results show, as *The X Factor* attracts some of the biggest names in pop. The contestants will also have the chance to work with celebrity mentors during the week leading up to the live show. These visiting singers work with the contestants and help them to improve their performances.

THE FINAL

Who will be the final contestant left standing onstage this year? There's only one way to find out!

97

AIDEN GRIMSHAW

UNDER 28 BOYS

Profile

Age:	18
Home town:	Blackpool
Job:	Student
Audition city:	Manchester
Mentor:	Dannii

"Now that's what I call a
POPSTAR!

Simon

A

iden had his first taste of stardom onstage in a school performance of Grease. But auditioning for *The X Factor* was his opportunity to step onto an international stage

After introducing himself to the Judges, Aiden's voice rang out with confidence and style. The audience started to clap, and then rose to its feet, applauding. They could tell that Aiden had something special.

After Bootcamp, he travelled to Australia to meet Dannii, who chose him for the live shows. He has come a long way from the days when he used to sing for his grandma, but can his journey take him all the way to the top?

"You have a lot of SOUL."
Nicole

"You've got your own SWAGGER."
Louis

"You are one of the BEST we've found."
Simon

YOU ARE THE FIFTH JUDGE!

JOIN THE JUDGING PANEL AND RECORD YOUR THOUGHTS ABOUT AIDEN'S PERFORMANCES.

BEST PERFORMANCE: Bootcamp

WEAKEST MOMENT: biggintraining

BEST OUTFIT: JUDGES houses day 1

NEEDS TO WORK ON: Nothing

DOES AIDEN HAVE THE X FACTOR? OF course

YOUR X FACTOR SCORE: 9/10

NICOLO FESTA

UNDER 28 BOYS

Profile

Age:	21
Home town:	Traviso
Job:	Student
Audition city:	London
Mentor:	Dannii

"There's something really **CHARMING** about you."

Cheryl

Nicolo

Nicolo has been dreaming of being a music legend for as long as he can remember. He truly believes that he could be the contestant who has everything – the look, the style, the attitude and the voice.

Nicolo wanted to use his audition to show the judges that he has the 'x factor'. When he began to sing, whistles echoed around the auditorium. Cheryl turned to Simon in excitement.

The young Italian has worked his way through Bootcamp and the Judges' Houses stage, and now he has the chance to sing his way to the final. Will Nicolo be the winner of *The X Factor* 2010?

JUDGES' HOUSES

"Everything about you is **DIFFERENT.**"
Louis

FIRST AUDITION

"I like you because you're **WEIRD.**"
Simon

JUDGES' HOUSES

"A real **DIVA!**"
Simon

YOU ARE THE FIFTH JUDGE!

JOIN THE JUDGING PANEL AND RECORD YOUR THOUGHTS ABOUT NICOLO'S PERFORMANCES.

BEST PERFORMANCE: first beformanse

WEAKEST MOMENT: None

BEST OUTFIT: Judeyges houses day 2

NEEDS TO WORK ON: high notes

DOES NICOLO HAVE THE X FACTOR? a little

YOUR X FACTOR SCORE: 8/10

MATT CARDLE

UNDER 28 BOYS

Profile

Age:	27
Home town:	Halstead
Job:	Painter & Decorator
Audition city:	London
Mentor:	Dannii

"**There's something QUIRKY and likeable about you.**"

Louis

Matt works as a painter, but he's thoroughly bored of redecorating hotel rooms. He's been thinking about auditioning for a long time, and this year he finally felt ready.

At audition stage in London, the audience was roaring approval as soon as Matt started singing. His unusual tone and laid-back look was a winning combination, and the Judges sent him straight to Bootcamp with three almighty yesses.

Matt is hoping that getting through to the live shows means the end of paintbrushes, hotel walls and magnolia paint. With Dannii as his mentor, can he make it all the way to the final?

JUDGES' HOUSES

"I am going to say YES!"
Cheryl

JUDGES' HOUSES

"I really really LIKE YOU."
Simon

JUDGES' HOUSES

"You're very MUSICAL."
Louis

YOU ARE THE FIFTH JUDGE!

JOIN THE JUDGING PANEL AND RECORD YOUR THOUGHTS ABOUT MATT'S PERFORMANCES.

BEST PERFORMANCE: first adishan

WEAKEST MOMENT: None

BEST OUTFIT: Judges houses day 3

NEEDS TO WORK ON: ~~know notes~~ nothing

DOES MATT HAVE THE X FACTOR? Yes

YOUR X FACTOR SCORE: 10/10

"There's something **SPECIAL** about you."

Simon

CHER LLOYD

UNDER 28 GIRLS

Profile

Age:	16
Home town:	Malvern
Job:	Student
Audition city:	Birmingham
Mentor:	Cheryl

6235

Cher's legs were shaking with nerves as she stepped out in front of the Judges. But as soon as the music started, her jitters seemed to disappear.

Suddenly she was a confident performer, her big eyes full of attitude as she strutted across the stage. The audience listened with rapt attention and gave her a standing ovation when her song ended.

Listening to the Judges' comments, tears of joy and amazement filled Cher's eyes. This was everything she had ever wanted. She was destined for Cheryl's house, where her performances persuaded her mentor to choose her for the live shows. Now her goal is in sight, and Cher is determined to make her dreams come true!

"You where born to be a POPSTAR."
Loius

"You are right UP MY STREET!"
Cheryl

"You've got SO MUCH potential."
Natalie

YOU ARE THE FIFTH JUDGE!

JOIN THE JUDGING PANEL AND RECORD YOUR THOUGHTS ABOUT CHER'S PERFORMANCES.

BEST PERFORMANCE: *First Adishon*

WEAKEST MOMENT: *Judges houses*

BEST OUTFIT: *all*

NEEDS TO WORK ON: *Nothing*

DOES CHER HAVE THE X FACTOR? *Yes*

YOUR X FACTOR SCORE: *10/10*

KATIE WAISSEL

UNDER 28 GIRLS

Profile

Age:	24
Home town:	North London
Job:	Receptionist
Audition city:	London
Mentor:	Cheryl

"You're quite likeable, you're quite CHARMING."

Simon

Katie has wanted to be onstage for as long as she can remember. She arrived at her audition hoping to really impress the Judges.

However, things didn't go according to plan – she forgot the words and had a couple of false starts. Things weren't looking good for Katie, but when she started to sing, it became clear that she had real talent.

Katie progressed through Bootcamp to the Judges' Houses stage, where she thoroughly impressed her mentor. She can't wait to step onto the *X Factor* stage and show the UK that she is the next big thing!

JUDGES' HOUSES

BOOTCAMP

JUDGES' HOUSES

"You've got your own
IDENTITY."
Cheryl

"I LOVE
your style."
Cheryl

YOU ARE THE FIFTH JUDGE!
JOIN THE JUDGING PANEL AND RECORD YOUR THOUGHTS ABOUT KATIE'S PERFORMANCES.

BEST PERFORMANCE: _all_

WEAKEST MOMENT: _None_

BEST OUTFIT: _all_

NEEDS TO WORK ON: _high notes_

DOES KATIE HAVE THE X FACTOR? _a little_

YOUR X FACTOR SCORE: _9_ /10

REBECCA FERGUSON

UNDER 28 GIRLS

Profile

Age:	23
Home town:	Liverpool
Job:	Student
Audition city:	Manchester
Mentor:	Cheryl

"You're voice really **MOVES ME.**"

Nicole

Rebecca was suffering from a severe lack of confidence when she arrived at *The X Factor* auditions in Manchester.

She has always believed that she was meant to be a singer, and that belief carried her to sing in front of the Judges.

Looking down shyly, Rebecca began to sing. As her beautiful voice rang out, the Judges and the audience listened breathlessly.

Everyone loved her voice, but Nicole pointed out that although it was OK to be vulnerable, she still had to connect with the audience.

Now that she is through to the live shows, can Rebecca find her confidence and be her true self onstage?

JUDGES' HOUSES

BOOTCAMP

"You've got three **YESSES!**"
Simon

"You have an **INCREDIBLE VOICE.**"
Simon

YOU ARE THE FIFTH JUDGE!
JOIN THE JUDGING PANEL AND RECORD YOUR THOUGHTS ABOUT REBECCA'S PERFORMANCES.

BEST PERFORMANCE: Bootcamp

WEAKEST MOMENT: None

BEST OUTFIT: all

NEEDS TO WORK ON: Nothing

DOES REBECCA HAVE THE X FACTOR? Yes ofcourse

YOUR X FACTOR SCORE: 10/10

FYD

GROUPS

Profile

Age:	**21-25**
Home towns:	**Fulham, Brixton, Llandudno, Woking, Birmingham**
Jobs:	**Dance Teachers, Dancers, Customer Support Co-ordinator**
Audition city:	**London**
Mentor:	**Simon**

"The progression from
when we first saw them to now is
STAGGERING."

Simon

F.Y.D., which stands for Find Your Destination, is made up of friends Kalvin LaMey, Alex Murdoch, Ryan-Lee Seager, Matt Newton and Jordan Gabriel

Singing 'She Said' they performed a slick song and dance routine that had Louis and Cheryl grinning. However, Simon was going to take a little more convincing. At Bootcamp, F.Y.D. seized their opportunity and proved to Simon that they could develop and learn at impressive speed. He was so impressed that when he found them in his category, he chose them to represent him at the live shows. F.Y.D. have faith in themselves and hope that their unique sound will take them to the final.

JUDGES' HOUSES

"One of the BEST GROUPS we have seen."
Simon

JUDGES' HOUSES

"They were so FUN."
Nicole

YOU ARE THE FIFTH JUDGE!

JOIN THE JUDGING PANEL AND RECORD YOUR THOUGHTS ABOUT F.Y.D.'S PERFORMANCES.

BEST PERFORMANCE: Judges Houses

WEAKEST MOMENT: None

BEST OUTFIT: all

NEEDS TO WORK ON: High notes

DO F.Y.D. HAVE THE X FACTOR? a little

YOUR X FACTOR SCORE: 9/10

BELLE AMIE

GROUPS

Profile

Age:	17 - 23
Home towns:	Dublin, London, Charlton, Scarborough
Job:	Students, Ex Hairdresser
Audition cities:	Dublin, London, Manchester
Mentor:	Simon

"Thank you for making this day a bit more **EXCITING.**"

Cheryl

Esther Campbell, Geneva Lane, Sophia Wardman and Rebecca Creighton were brought together at Bootcamp to form a brand-new girl band – Belle Amie.

All four girls did well at audition stage and were impressive at Bootcamp. When the Judges suggested that their voices would blend together well, the girls rose to the challenge, creating a great sound and believable chemistry in the space of three days.

Belle Amie are massively excited to have made it all the way to the live shows, and hope to prove to the nation that the Judges have made the right decision in creating the group.

FIRST AUDITION

"You're **LIKEABLE.**"
Nicole

FIRST AUDITION

"Something **CUTE** about you."
Cheryl

FIRST AUDITION

"You have a **TWINKLE** in your eye."
Nicole

FIRST AUDITION

"You look like a **LITTLE POPSTAR.**"
Simon

YOU ARE THE FIFTH JUDGE!

JOIN THE JUDGING PANEL AND RECORD YOUR THOUGHTS ABOUT BELLE AMIE'S PERFORMANCES.

BEST PERFORMANCE: *all*

WEAKEST MOMENT: *none*

BEST OUTFIT: *all*

NEEDS TO WORK ON: *nothing*

DO BELLE AMIE HAVE THE X FACTOR? *Yes*

YOUR X FACTOR SCORE: *10/10*

1DIRECTION

GROUPS

Profile

Age:	16 - 18
Home towns:	Mullinger, Doncaster, Birmingham, Holmes Chapel, Bradford
Job:	Students
Audition cities:	Dublin, Manchester, Birmingham
Mentor:	Simon

"That was **EXTRAORDINARY.**"

Simon

Like Belle Amie, 1Direction came together at Bootcamp after the Judges suggested that they would make a fantastic group.

Harry Styles, Niall Horan, Liam Payne, Louis Tomlinson and Zain Malik poured their energy into learning how to harmonise together, and made it to the Judges' Houses stage.

It's not the first time that the Judges have suggested that contestants should join forces.

Last year girl band Miss F.R.A.N.K. was created at the Judges' suggestion. This time, the Judges were hugely excited to be behind the creation of a new boy band.

Now that they are through to the live shows, it's up to the boys to show that they are a winning combination.

"Your voice is POWERFUL."
Cheryl

FIRST AUDITION

FIRST AUDITION

FIRST AUDITION

FIRST AUDITION

"He's a CONTENDER."
Louis

FIRST AUDITION

YOU ARE THE FIFTH JUDGE!

JOIN THE JUDGING PANEL AND RECORD YOUR THOUGHTS ABOUT 1DIRECTION'S PERFORMANCES.

BEST PERFORMANCE: all

WEAKEST MOMENT: None

BEST OUTFIT: all

NEEDS TO WORK ON: high notes

DO 1DIRECTION HAVE THE X FACTOR? yes

YOUR X FACTOR SCORE: 10/10

JOHN ADELEYE

OVER 28'S

Profile

Age:	29
Home town:	London
Job:	Activity Coordinator
Audition city:	London
Mentor:	Louis

"Nice guy, honest guy, GREAT VOICE."

Simon

John organises activities for patients with memory problems. His eyes sparkle when he talks about the sense of satisfaction his work brings him.

But there is another dream in his heart and he came along to his audition hoping that *The X Factor* would make it come true.

Smiling and relaxed, John's audition charmed all the Judges. His smile lit up the stage and his voice had the audience cheering and applauding.

Having sung his way to the Judges' Houses stage, Louis chose John as one of his contestants in the live shows. He has worked hard to get this far, but there is still a long way to go!

BOOTCAMP

"You are what it says
ON THE TIN."
Simon

FIRST AUDITION

"Something really
ADORABLE
about you."
Cheryl

JUDGES' HOUSES

"You've got
a really, really
GREAT voice."
Louis

YOU ARE THE FIFTH JUDGE!

JOIN THE JUDGING PANEL AND RECORD YOUR THOUGHTS ABOUT JOHN'S PERFORMANCES.

BEST PERFORMANCE: *all*

WEAKEST MOMENT: *None*

BEST OUTFIT: *Bootcamp*

NEEDS TO WORK ON: *nothing*

DOES JOHN HAVE THE X FACTOR? *a little*

YOUR X FACTOR SCORE: *8* /10

MARY BYRNE

OVER 28'S

Profile

Age:	50
Home town:	Dublin
Job:	Supermarket worker
Audition city:	Dublin
Mentor:	Louis

"**MY FAVOURITE**
audition of Dublin."

Cheryl

Mary approached her audition with her nerves jangling. It had taken her a long time to build up the confidence to stand in front of the Judges.

As soon as she began to sing, Mary's powerful voice captivated the Judges and the audience. Her singing was rich with emotion, and people jumped spontaneously to their feet, roaring their approval.

Hardly able to believe that she had made it to Bootcamp, Mary went on to prove over and over again that she deserved a place in the live shows. Can she maintain her rise towards stardom and get the public voting for her?

BOOTCAMP

"Seriously, seriously
GOOD!"
Simon

JUDGES' HOUSES

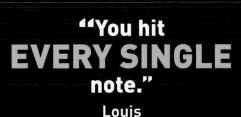

"You hit
EVERY SINGLE
note."
Louis

JUDGES' HOUSES

YOU ARE THE FIFTH JUDGE!
JOIN THE JUDGING PANEL AND RECORD YOUR THOUGHTS ABOUT MARY'S PERFORMANCES.

BEST PERFORMANCE: *all*

WEAKEST MOMENT: *None*

BEST OUTFIT: *Judges houses day 2*

NEEDS TO WORK ON: *high notes*

DOES MARY HAVE THE X FACTOR? *a little*

YOUR X FACTOR SCORE: *9/10*

STORM LEE

OVER 28'S

Profile

Age:	37
Home town:	Los Angeles
Job:	Singer / Songwriter
Audition city:	London
Mentor:	Louis

"Your voice was really FANTASTIC."

Cheryl

Storm feels that he has a gift. He's hoping that *The X Factor* is the platform that will allow him to share his gift with the world.

However, his audition did not go smoothly. Simon stopped him and asked him to sing a different song. It was obvious that the outspoken Judge had his doubts. But Storm closed his eyes and focused on singing the song that could change his life.

Storm made it to Bootcamp and then to the Judges' Houses stage, where Louis chose him to appear in the live shows. Now it is up to Storm to repay Louis's trust. Will he be this year's winner?

JUDGES' HOUSES

"**I think you DESERVE a chance.**"
Louis

FIRST AUDITION

"**I think you've got a GREAT VOICE.**"
Louis

BOOTCAMP

YOU ARE THE FIFTH JUDGE!
JOIN THE JUDGING PANEL AND RECORD YOUR THOUGHTS ABOUT STORM'S PERFORMANCES.

BEST PERFORMANCE: Judges houses

WEAKEST MOMENT: None

BEST OUTFIT: Judges houses

NEEDS TO WORK ON: lots

DOES STORM HAVE THE X FACTOR? a ting b it

YOUR X FACTOR SCORE: 7/10

MEET THE FINALISTS

WILDCARD

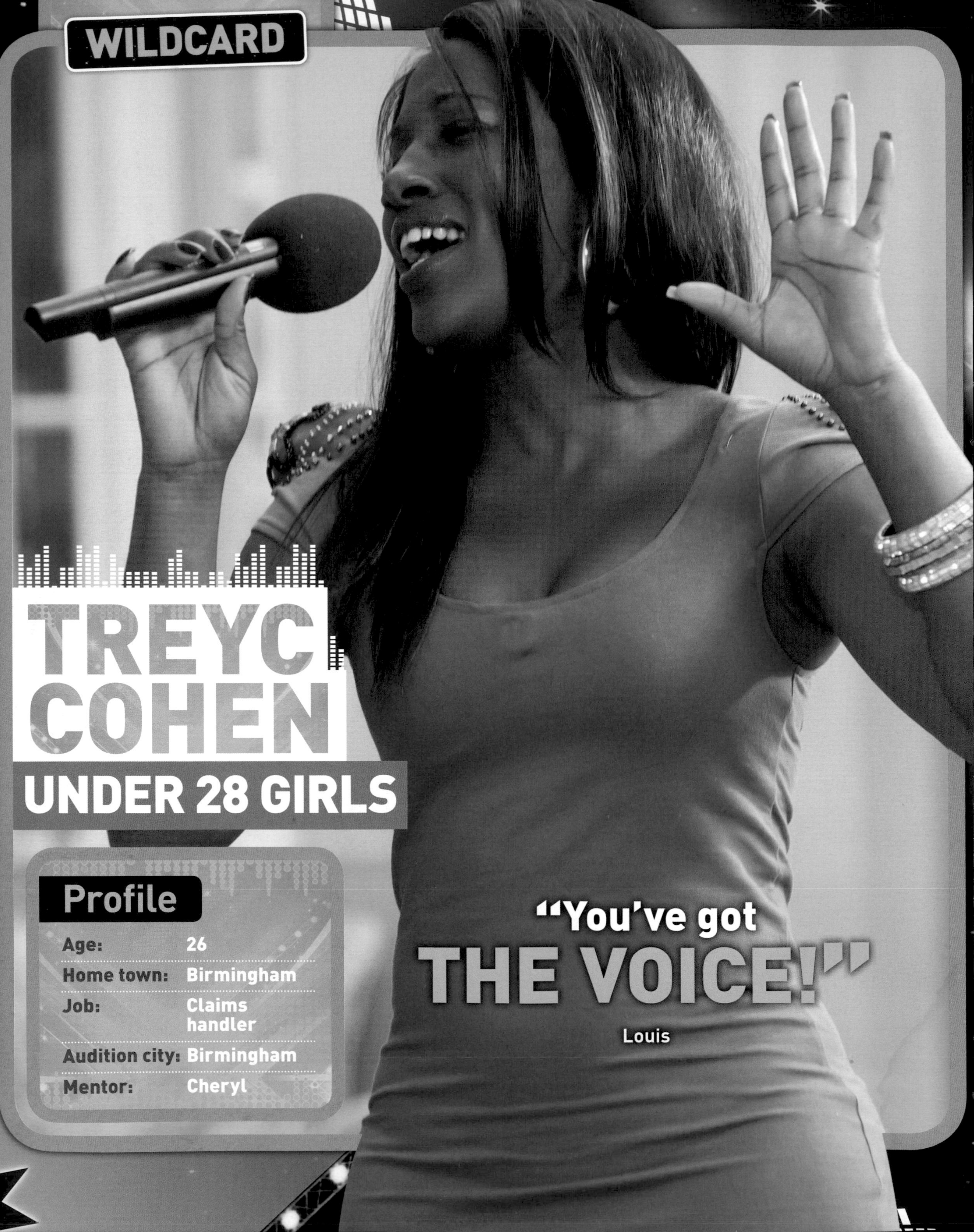

TREYC COHEN

UNDER 28 GIRLS

Profile

Age:	26
Home town:	Birmingham
Job:	Claims handler
Audition city:	Birmingham
Mentor:	Cheryl

"You've got **THE VOICE!**"

Louis

Treyc originally auditioned for last year's show, and made it all the way to the Judges' Houses stage. She wasn't put through to the live shows, but she refused to accept defeat.

Treyc arrived at this year's auditions with a new look and a new sense of purpose.

The Judges were impressed with Treyc's improvement and performance, and chose to put her through to Bootcamp. She went on to the Judges' Houses stage, and the last-minute shake-up gave her a place in the live shows. Now it's up to Treyc to prove that she deserves a place in the final.

BOOTCAMP

"She's like a DIFFERENT PERSON."
Simon

FIRST AUDITION

"Nice to have you BACK."
Simon

JUDGES' HOUSES

YOU ARE THE FIFTH JUDGE!

JOIN THE JUDGING PANEL AND RECORD YOUR THOUGHTS ABOUT TREYC'S PERFORMANCES.

BEST PERFORMANCE: Bootcamp Yes

WEAKEST MOMENT: None

BEST OUTFIT: Bootcamp Houses

NEEDS TO WORK ON: Nothing

DOES TREYC HAVE THE X FACTOR? Yes

YOUR X FACTOR SCORE: 10/10

WILDCARD

WAGNER FIUZA-CARRILHO

OVER 28'S

Profile

Age:	54
Home town:	Birmingham
Job:	Retired P.E. Teacher
Audition city:	Birmingham
Mentor:	Louis

"My mum would really, really **FANCY YOU!**"

Simon

Wagner charmed the Judges and the audience with his friendly manner and his unique style.

When he started singing, it was obvious that he had a special gift. As his powerful voice rang out, people in the audience punched the air and cheered. Simon was smiling and applauding.

Wagner rose to the challenges of Bootcamp and impressed the Judges with his energy and enthusiasm. He kept up the spirits of the other contestants and made it through to the Judges' Houses stage. Now Wagner is heading to the live shows as one of the final sixteen contestants. He has a chance in a million – can he make his dreams a reality?

"He's DIFFERENT."
Nicole

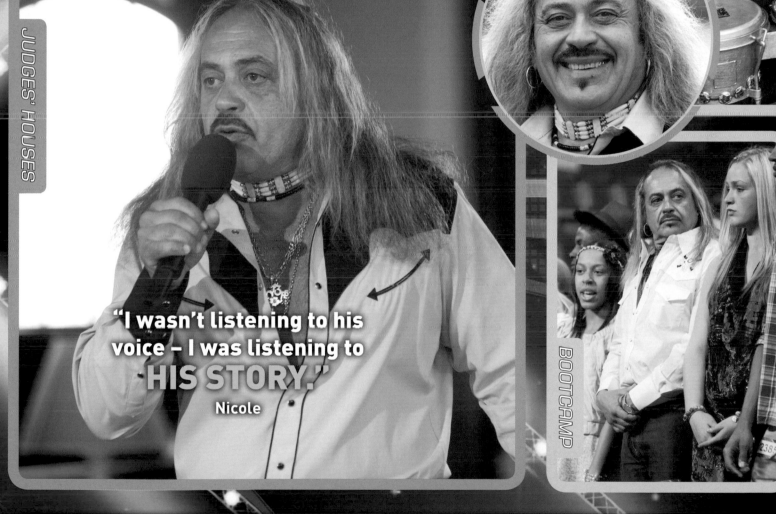

"I wasn't listening to his voice – I was listening to **HIS STORY."**
Nicole

YOU ARE THE FIFTH JUDGE!
JOIN THE JUDGING PANEL AND RECORD YOUR THOUGHTS ABOUT WAGNER'S PERFORMANCES.

BEST PERFORMANCE: *None*

WEAKEST MOMENT: *all*

BEST OUTFIT: *None*

NEEDS TO WORK ON: *everything*

DOES WAGNER HAVE THE X FACTOR? *No*

YOUR X FACTOR SCORE: *1* /10

DIVA FEVER

GROUPS

Profile

Age:	21 & 26
Home towns:	Leicester & Peterborough
Job:	Student/ Customer services assistant
Audition city:	Manchester
Mentor:	Simon

"People **LOVE**
a bit of camp"

Louis

Josef and Craig had Nicole on her feet and dancing with their fantastic audition performance of 'Proud Mary'. The audience appreciated their cheeky humour and were delighted when the Judges put them through to Bootcamp.

The boys knew that they had a lot of work ahead of them if they were going to keep their dreams of stardom alive. They did well at Bootcamp and made it to the Judges' Houses stage, where they were excited to discover that Simon would be their mentor.

Now that they have reached the live shows, they must deliver fabulous performances week after week to be in with a chance of winning the competition. Can Diva Fever make it to the final?

"You're **FUN.**"
Simon

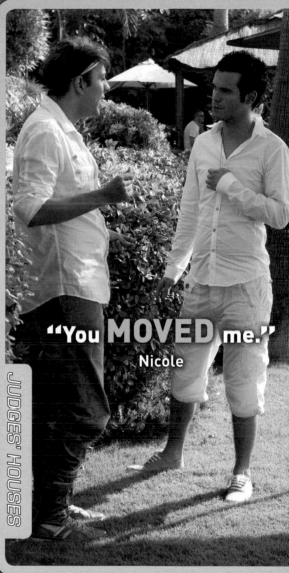

"You **MOVED** me."
Nicole

YOU ARE THE FIFTH JUDGE!

JOIN THE JUDGING PANEL AND RECORD YOUR THOUGHTS ABOUT DIVA FEVER'S PERFORMANCES.

BEST PERFORMANCE: Judges houses

WEAKEST MOMENT: None

BEST OUTFIT: Judges houses

NEEDS TO WORK ON: high notes

DOES DIVA FEVER HAVE THE X FACTOR? Yes

YOUR X FACTOR SCORE: 10/10

80534

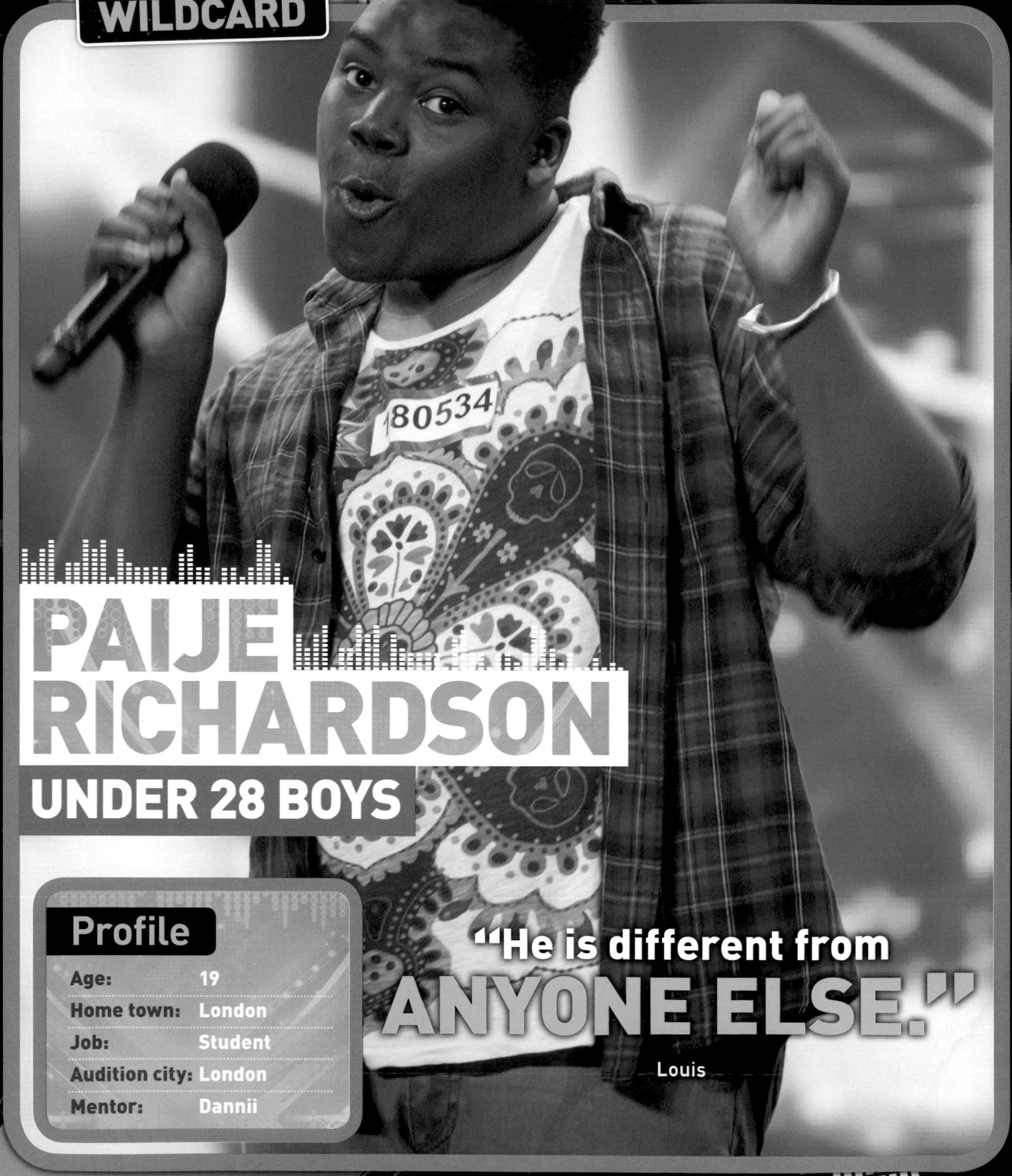

PAIJE RICHARDSON

UNDER 28 BOYS

Profile

Age:	19
Home town:	London
Job:	Student
Audition city:	London
Mentor:	Dannii

"He is different from ANYONE ELSE."

Louis

Paije's rich jazz voice has made him a firm favourite with the voting public. However, he almost didn't make it through the first stage of the competition!

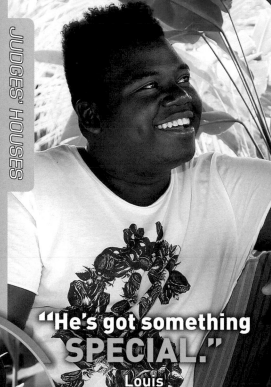

Paije's first audition completely split the Judges. Although his performance was popular with the audience, Cheryl and Simon were not convinced. However, Louis persuaded the other Judges to give him a second chance.

Paije's second audition wowed Cheryl and Simon, while the audience gave him a standing ovation. The Judges unanimously agreed to put him through to Bootcamp, and Paije was overjoyed.

At the Judges' Houses stage, he put his heart and soul into his performances, and his efforts were rewarded. Can he maintain his high standard and make his dreams come true?

"He's got something SPECIAL."
Louis

JUDGES' HOUSES

"He is a DIVA."
Simon

JUDGES' HOUSES

YOU ARE THE FIFTH JUDGE!

JOIN THE JUDGING PANEL AND RECORD YOUR THOUGHTS ABOUT PAIJE'S PERFORMANCES.

BEST PERFORMANCE: *Boot camp*

WEAKEST MOMENT: *None*

BEST OUTFIT: *Judges houses*

NEEDS TO WORK ON: *Nothing*

DOES PAIJE HAVE THE X FACTOR? *Yes*

YOUR X FACTOR SCORE: *10*/10

JOE MCELDERRY

SERIES 6 **WINNER**

Fact File

Name:	**Joseph McElderry**
D.O.B:	**16/06/91**
Home Town:	**South Shields**
Singing Style:	**Pop**

"Absolutely BRILLIANT."

Simon

Audition

Joe auditioned in Manchester and sang 'Dance With My Father'. He grew up listening to Luther Vandross, and felt confident that he could give a strong performance.

His song was filled with warmth and emotion, and his personality quickly won the hearts of the audience. They rose to their feet at the end of the song, and the Judges were extremely impressed. Joe sailed through to Bootcamp with four yesses.

"You are SUCH A NICE GUY."

Simon

The Live Performances

Cheryl was Joe's mentor and chose him as one of her contestants in the live shows. In his very first week he met Robbie Williams, who gave him some valuable tips and advice. He went on to sing 'No Regrets', and to impress the Judges once again.

As the weeks went by, Joe's confidence and ability grew and developed. He made his performances seem effortless, although he was rehearsing and practising whenever he could. He took all stresses and challenges in his stride, and always sang from the heart.

Alongside the stresses of the competition, Joe was having to get used to the media attention. Fans waited for his autograph outside the house and cameras followed him wherever he went.

Despite this pressure, Joe continued to stay strong and focused. Just when the Judges thought he couldn't get any better, he would light up the stage with another improvement on the previous week's performance.

Winning Song
LIST

1.   'No Regrets'
2.   'Where Do Broken Hearts Go'
3.   'Sway'
4.   'Don't Stop Believin''
5.   'Circle of Life'
6.   'Somebody To Love'
7.   'Don't Let The Sun Go Down On Me'
8.   'Could It Be Magic'
9.   'Sorry Seems To Be The Hardest Word'
10. 'She's Out Of My Life'
11. 'Open Arms'
12. 'Dance With My Father'

"I couldn't BE PROUDER OF YOU."

Cheryl

The Final

Joe worked steadily and unstoppably towards the final. When he reached it, he proved once and for all what an incredible performer he is. His performances showed the millions of people watching that he truly deserved to win, and they voted accordingly. Over ten million people picked up the phone to make their choice.

When he was declared the winner over Olly Murs, Joe leapt into the air, shouting in surprise and delight. His eyes wide with shock, he could hardly catch his breath. The competition was over, but his journey had only just begun.

"You've got GREAT STAGE PRESENCE."
Louis

What Happened Next...

Joe's first single, 'The Climb' reached number one in the UK chart and was nominated for a BRIT Award. With his debut album due for release in autumn 2010, Joe's future is looking very bright!

WINNER 2010

WHO DO YOU PREDICT WILL HAVE THE DETERMINATION, TALENT AND STAR QUALITY TO WIN THIS YEAR'S X FACTOR?

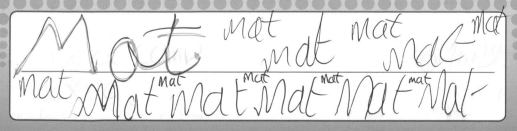

JLS

SERIES 5

"You've got
FANTASTIC CHEMISTRY!"

Louis

Marvin   Oritsé   Aston   JB

Biography

Oritsé Williams, Marvin Humes, Aston Merrygold and Jonathan "JB" Gill formed JLS out of a shared dream – to create the biggest and best boy band in the world.

The JLS boys have a wide variety of skills, including playing football and acting. But their hearts lie in the world of music.

They were already a band before they auditioned for the show, but being on *The X Factor* taught them valuable lessons and gave them the chance to sing to the British public. They became the most successful group of all time to enter *The X Factor*.

Unlike many other boy bands, JLS are involved in every part of the

creative process of making an album, and that's exactly the way they like it. The four boys have worked very hard to make their shared dream become a reality, and that hard work has paid off. Although they didn't win *The X Factor*, the show was their first step on the path to stardom and success.

The X Factor Experience

As Louis Walsh's only remaining group, JLS made it all the way to the final, having got the highest number of votes in the semi-finals. They were competing against Alexandra Burke, who went on to win. On the night, JLS sang their version of the winner's song, 'Hallelujah'.

Most Memorable Moment

In week nine, JLS performed 'Umbrella' and 'I'm Already There'. The Judges were full of praise. The boys were delighted when Simon told them "You could actually win this".

What Happened Next...

Following their success on *The X Factor*, JLS were signed up by Epic Records. Their first two singles went to number one on the UK Singles Chart.

JLS released their first album in 2009. It was the sixth best selling album in the UK during that year, and the first single to be released went to number one. In 2010 JLS won a BRIT Award – the first *X Factor* contestants to do so. Their next album is due for release in late 2010.

"I am in the
JLS FAN CLUB."
Cheryl

ALEXANDRA BURKE

SERIES 5

Biography

Alexandra Burke was determined to build a career in music as soon as she left school. That ambition led her to find work as a singer, and she was gigging in clubs before she auditioned for *The X Factor*.

She first auditioned for the show in 2005 but was unsuccessful. However, she worked hard on developing her talent, and tried again three years later. This time, with the help and guidance of Cheryl Cole, she made it through to the live shows.

"You LOOK LIKE A DIVA."

Louis

The X Factor Experience

Alexandra was consistent and impressive throughout the live shows, and received the first of many standing ovations in week three. Mariah Carey praised her voice and as the live shows progressed she became favourite to win.

In the final, Alexandra sang a superb duet with Beyoncé, which was a dream come true for her. It must have felt like a fairytale, but it was Alexandra's hard work and dedication that had brought her so far. Her reward was to be named the winner of *The X Factor* 2008.

"I LOVE YOU to bits."
Cheryl

Most Memorable Moment

With Mariah Carey just a few feet away, Alexandra sang 'Without You' so magnificently that she brought the Judges to their feet.

Wearing a shimmering golden gown, she entranced the audience with the power and emotion of her performance.

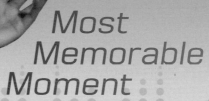

What happened Next...

Alexandra's first single was the Christmas number one in 2008 and the top-selling song of the year. Her first album was released the following year and entered the charts at number one. She has been nominated for two BRIT Awards and has done a lot of work for charity. Alexandra has performed on the Royal Variety Show and become the face of a fashion line. She has even reappeared on *The X Factor* in 2009 – this time as a guest star! Her European Promo Tour began in 2010.

LEONA LEWIS

SERIES 3

Biography

The shy yet dazzling winner of *The X Factor* 2006 was born and brought up in London, and dreamed of being a singer from a very young age. After leaving school she worked hard to get a recording contract, but it wasn't until she auditioned for *The X Factor* that her music career really took off.

She was afraid of being knocked back, but despite her nerves something spurred her on to believe that she could make her dreams come true.

"You are ABSOLUTELY THE BEST contestant I have ever had!"

Simon

The X Factor Experience

From the moment she auditioned, it was clear that Leona had an extraordinary singing voice. The Judges were clearly excited, and she progressed steadily through the Bootcamp and Judges' Houses stages, deeply impressing her mentor Simon.

As the live shows stretched and tested the competitors, Leona showed that she had the talent and the commitment to rise to any challenge. Week after week she sang her heart out, and viewers voted for her in their thousands.

Leona's confidence in herself grew, but she could hardly believe that she had made it to the final. She gave a sensational final performance, and became the third winner of *The X Factor*.

"You're a CLASS ACT"

Louis

Most Memorable Moment

Leona's performance of 'Summertime' in week three was an astonishing achievement that completely raised the roof. Her outstanding voice and warm personality had already made her a firm favourite in the hearts of the nation.

When she performed 'I Will Always Love You' a few weeks later, she had not only the audience but also the Judges on their feet. Her love of singing shone through and created an unforgettable piece of television history.

What happened Next...

After spectacular performances at the final, Leona won the series and went on to have the Christmas number one, which was also the most downloaded song of 2006. Her first album was the fastest-selling debut album and the biggest seller of 2007 in the UK.

Leona has broken all sorts of records, including becoming the first British artist to reach number one in the US with a debut album. Her second album was released in 2009 and reached number one in the UK Albums Chart. In 2010 she went on her first tour and is now working on her third album.

OLLY *MURS*
Series 6

"You're very, VERY COOL."
— Simon

Olly was a star striker in his school's football team, but his heart's desire was to become a pop star. He auditioned for *The X Factor* in 2009, and his performance of 'Superstition' massively impressed the Judges. Simon Cowell said it was the easiest 'yes' he had ever given.

After doing well in the early stages of the competition, Olly gained Simon as his mentor and was chosen to appear in the live shows. He reached the live finals, although he was in the bottom two in week seven. During the final he sang a duet with his idol Robbie Williams, and went on to achieve second place.

Since his appearance on the show, Olly has had a busy year. He has performed on *The X Factor* Live tour, and has also performed gigs across the UK. Olly released his debut single in August 2010. 'Please Don't Let Me Go' went straight to number one in the UK singles charts. His first album is due for release towards the tend of 2010.

OLLY'S SONG LIST

1. 'She's the One'
2. 'A Fool in Love'
3. 'Bewitched'
4. 'Come Together'
5. 'Twist and Shout'
6. 'Don't Stop Me Now'
7. 'Fastlove'
8. 'Love Ain't Here Any More'
9. 'Saturday Night's Alright for Fighting'
10. 'Can You Feel It'
11. 'We Can Work It Out'
12. 'Superstition'

DIANA VICKERS
Series 5

Diana began singing when she was eleven, but her first experience of what it meant to sing professionally came when she auditioned for *The X Factor* in 2008.

Her unique singing style made her one of the most talked-about contestants in the show. She created headlines when she missed the live show in week five, because she was suffering from laryngitis. It was the first time in the show's history that an act had been excused from performing.

In a shock twist, Diana was voted out of the show in week nine, despite being the Bookies' favourite to win. However, the UK had not seen the last of the kooky performer.

Diana was part of *The X Factor* Live tour and went on to sign a record deal in 2009. She immediately began work on her debut album, 'Songs from the Tainted Cherry Tree', which achieved the number-one place in the UK Albums Chart. Her first single, 'Once', also reached number one.

Between 2009 and 2010, Diana gave an award-winning performance in *The Rise and Fall of Little Voice*. In March 2010, she began her first official UK tour. She has also appeared in various music festivals, including the V Festival and the Live Lounge Stage at Radio 1's Big Weekend. What will 2011 bring for this rising star?

DIANA'S SONG LIST

1. 'With or Without You'
2. 'Man in the Mirror'
3. 'Smile'
4. 'Call Me'
5. 'Yellow'
6. 'Patience'
7. 'I'm Not a Girl, Not Yet A Woman'
8. 'Everybody Hurts'
9. 'Girlfriend'
10. 'White Flag'

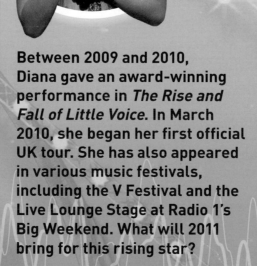